D1305999

A Student's Guide to

TENNESSEE
WILLIAMS

A Student's Guide to

TENNESSEE WILLIAMS

Spring Hermann

Enslow Publishers, Inc.
40 Industrial Road
Box 398
Berkeley Heights, NJ 07922
USA

http://www.enslow.com

Library of Congress Cataloging-in-Publication Data

Hermann, Spring.
    A student's guide to Tennessee Williams / Spring Hermann.
        p. cm. — (Understanding literature)
    Includes bibliographical references and index.
    ISBN-13: 978-0-7660-2706-0
    ISBN-10: 0-7660-2706-6
    1. Williams, Tennessee, 1911–1983—Criticism and interpretation—Juvenile literature. I. Title. II. Title: Tennessee Williams.
    PS3545.I5365Z677 2005
    812'.54—dc22

                                                    2006036458

Printed in the United States of America

10 9 8 7 6 5 4 3 2 1

To Our Readers: We have done our best to make sure all Internet Addresses in this book were active and appropriate when we went to press. However, the author and the publisher have no control over and assume no liability for the material available on those Internet sites or on other Web sites they may link to. Any comments or suggestions can be sent by e-mail to comments@enslow.com or to the address on the back cover.

Illustration Credits: AP/Wide World Photos, p. 112; Everett Collection, Inc., pp. 49, 59; by Permission of the Houghton Library, Harvard University, pp. 19, 30, 45, 85; Photo courtesy of Spring Hermann, pp. 72, 130.

Cover Illustration: By Permission of the Houghton Library, Harvard University (inset); Corel Corporation/ Hemera Technologies, Inc./ Everett Collection, Inc. (background objects).

Dedication

In Memory of my mother, Margaret F. Hermann, who made me her theatre companion and devotee of the stage since childhood;

And for The Playreading Group: Betty and Herb Hoffman, Marj and Mel Johnson, Vicky and Charlie Beristain, Victor and Ruth Finizio, Rosemary Winandy, and my husband Vincent, who share with me the joy of reading aloud works of great dramatic literature.

SPECIAL THANKS: To Christopher Baker and the Hartford Stage Company for their kind assistance to this book, and for their devotion to presenting the entire canon of Tennessee Williams.

CONTENTS

A PLAYWRIGHT IS BORN

An introduction to the life and works of Tennessee Williams

om Williams arrived in St. Louis, the city that had been his home since he was seven. He had left his studies at the University of Iowa and rushed back for an important reason. His play was "going up," to the delight of his family, friends, and community.

The Mummers of Saint Louis, a community theater, would present the premiere of *Fugitive Kind* by Thomas Lanier Williams. The play would have two performances, Tuesday, November 30, and Saturday, December 4, 1937, in the Wednesday Club Auditorium.

The Mummers had also done Williams's first play, *Candles to the Sun*, in January 1937. This play about downtrodden coal miners used the sun to symbolize group consciousness and labor-union power. It was not a play that remained popular. However, it was "a local success."[1]

It encouraged the Mummers to believe in Williams as a writer of realistic social drama.

Tom Williams had finished the draft of *Fugitive Kind*, his second full-length play, in September, just before he took the train to Iowa City. He hoped to finish his undergraduate degree in English and theater at the University of Iowa. Although he had completed three years of work at the University of Missouri, he had spent too much of his time in his fraternity house, writing or drinking. He either dropped or failed necessary courses, such as physical education and ROTC. This so angered his father, Cornelius C. Williams, that he refused to pay for his son's senior year.

In truth, C. C. Williams, although employed, still had money difficulties in 1932, due to America's deep economic depression. He insisted that his son drop out of college and take a job at his business, International Shoe Company. Tom Williams hated every day of corporate work. His job, however, never stopped him from writing all night instead of sleeping. Looking back, he remembered his positions at International Shoe: "They tried me at everything. I was a miracle of incompetence."[2] Factory work made him so depressed he became physically ill. Finally, his father let him quit.

At age twenty-six, Tom Williams needed one last chance to finish his college degree. His mother and grandparents scrimped to send him to Iowa City, where the University of Iowa was famous for its theater department. When he left for college, he wrote in his journal about

Fugitive Kind: "My play is all but finished and I feel pretty well satisfied with it. Now I yearn for work on a new one. . . . The next play is always the important play. . . . I want to go on creating. I will!"[3]

Now Tom Williams walked the wintry streets of St. Louis on his way to the Mummer's theater rehearsal. During the year, after leaving International Shoe, he had tried working at a few low-paying jobs across the country. He encountered troubled people enduring human dilemmas. In *Fugitive Kind*, he had brought these people to life.

TOM WILLIAMS'S CHARACTERS MOVE FROM LIFE TO THE STAGE

Most of the characters in *Fugitive Kind* were homeless. They lived in a cheap transient hotel called a flophouse. Williams actually explored some of these flophouses to gain a true perspective. The Depression of the 1930s and the unsympathetic large corporations (such as International Shoe, in his mind) had forced millions of Americans into marginal lives. He tried to tell their stories. The characters in *Fugitive Kind* also experience the threat of crime and the presence of a robber on the run. Tom Williams knew that his audiences would relate to underprivileged people who broke the law. Criminals were almost folk heroes during the Depression.

Williams had introduced a large cast of twenty-five

diverse individuals. Many of these characters were briefly seen and provided background material. Others were deeply portrayed. All of his characters had a style of speaking that perfectly suited their background and role in life. He even spelled out the European Jewish accent one character needed when writing his speeches. These characters spoke using internal and external monologues. Some of these monologues were more poetic than realistic.

MONOLOGUE (INTERNAL OR INTERIOR)—*A long speech by an individual character in which he lets the audience alone know his inner thoughts and feelings.*

MONOLOGUE (EXTERNAL OR EXTERIOR)—*A long speech by an individual character, sometimes in the presence of other characters, that reveals his past or planned actions and intentions.*

METAPHOR AND SYMBOL IN REALISTIC DRAMA

Tom Williams had been a poet first, then a short-story writer, and then a playwright. His impulse was to use *metaphors* in his plays, just as he did in his poetry. For him, a metaphor meant that locales and events stood for or symbolized something else.

In *Fugitive Kind*, his homeless characters move in and out of Gwendlebaum's flophouse for fifteen cents a night. He locates the flophouse near the banks of the Mississippi and the Eads Bridge. The bridge can be a metaphor for the way out of town, the way to get from a bad place to a better one. Williams himself was trying to use his playwriting as a bridge to get out of a dreary life with his oppressive parents into a world where he could achieve. However, he used the Eads Bridge as a site for an attempted suicide for Leo, a good but confused character in his play.

> **METAPHOR**—*An implied comparison achieved by using a word or phrase not in its literal sense, but as an analogy. Example (from Shakespeare): "Life's but a walking shadow, a poor player that struts and frets his hour upon the stage."*

Williams used the metaphor of snow, which looks white and pure and beautiful. Snow can disguise the mud of the world. His homeless characters also realize this same snow can freeze you to death. The regular ringing of a nearby cathedral's bells marks the passage of time.

> **SYMBOL**—*Something that stands for, represents, or suggests another thing.*
> **SYMBOLISM**—*The representation of things by use of symbols.*

The tolling of bells also symbolizes a march toward a dark, inevitable fate. The use of metaphoric locales and events with double interpretations would continue through Williams's works.

RELATIONSHIPS SEEN IN A NEW LIGHT

Another subject that Tom Williams explored in *Fugitive Kind* was *sexual attraction* between characters. In the 1930s, frank portrayal of people's sexual lives was not often seen on stage. Glory, the heroine of the play, is torn between two men. One is her safe, undemanding boyfriend, Herman. The other is a man on the run from a bank robbery gone badly. This man, Terry, is sophisticated, powerful, lonely, and appealing. Glory is hopelessly drawn to Terry. When the tension and desire between them become overwhelming, Glory succumbs to Terry sexually. She then plans their escape before the law catches him.

Williams would continue to develop *fascinating female characters*. Women with their own needs, intellects, and sexual desires would stand up to their male counterparts. As seen in the character of Glory, passion may cause women to make self-destructive mistakes. Yet Williams's female characters would follow their own impulsive drives.

WHY WE BECOME WHO WE ARE

In *Fugitive Kind*, Terry the criminal talks about the way *childhood traumas* and genetics influence the way we turn out as adults. In Scene 5, Terry tells Glory he was born with two strikes against him. His mother became a prostitute and got tuberculosis. As for his father, Terry tells Glory: "Maybe if my old man hadn't caught a steel rivet between the eyes when I was ten months old, I'd have turned out to be Herman."[4] Williams would consider how early family life shapes human development. In *Fugitive*

Kind, early nurturing seems a much stronger way to determine behavior than genetics.

ALTERNATIVE DRAMATIC SPEAKING STYLES

Terry delivers his feelings in an *interior monologue*. This device of a character revealing his inner thoughts allowed Williams to infuse poetry and emotion into ordinary speech. Terry also delivers *exterior monologues* to explain his situation. The other characters on stage, as well as the audience, could decide how they felt about the speaker. These techniques, often used in poetry and stories, would be effective in this play.

In one of the stage directions in *Fugitive Kind*, Williams tells the director: "Chuck's speeches will remain upon the realistic plane, but Leo's will really be passages of poetry and will have to be delivered as such."[5] The use of *poetic dialogue* would become a Williams trademark.

FINDING OUR PLACE IN THE WORLD

The theme of the *artist against the mechanistic world* is voiced in *Fugitive Kind*. The theme of what poets, artists, and performers, even dreamers, had to do to survive in America's business-oriented society was one close to Williams's heart. He hated the life of a daily clock puncher. Glory's brother, Leo, does not fit into routine corporate work. He says: "Why don't I belong out there with the rest of those people? . . . The only thing I'm good for, Chuck, is putting words down on paper. And what's the use of that?"[6]

REALISM—*A style of writing in which the subject is represented as it would be in real life.*

Tom would look at the idea of *dual realities*. One reality would be a situation as seen by the average working person. The second reality would be the same situation as perceived by the artistic dreamer. Which view of the situation is more "real"? Williams's characters would show that memory is seated in the heart, where it is strongly influenced by emotion.

MIND AND SPIRIT ARE EXPLORED

Tom Williams explores the relationship between God and mankind in *Fugitive Kind*. Williams and his sister, Rose, had spent their early years in the home of their grandfather, Reverend Walter Edwin Dakin, an Episcopal priest. Williams's mother, Edwina, taught a firm Christianity to her children. Yet Williams often wondered aloud in his writing whether God really cared. So many people seemed to suffer needlessly. A character in *Fugitive Kind* describes a world going to war while "God's asleep." A search for spiritual meaning would be made by many of Williams's characters. Later, guilt and the quest for salvation would become a recurring theme in his plays.

Another theme of his was only touched upon: the effect of depression and mental illness. Abel White, a transient, is a dangerous psychopath who starts fires. Glory's brother, Leo, an intense college student, becomes obsessed with Socialist politics. When the state of the world overwhelms him, Leo almost commits suicide. This theme of depression will reoccur in later plays.

While waiting for the Mummers's opening performance of *Fugitive Kind*, Williams himself became depressed. He had been promised a set that would show the oppressive city skyline and the falling snow through a huge window. This set did not materialize. His characters were not looking like fugitives crowded together in their last refuge. Williams suddenly feared that no one would relate to the characters or would understand the play's meaning. Nerves, fright, and loneliness were his devastating feelings on opening night. He would explore these emotional states through his characters.

A cast member of *Fugitive Kind*, Jane Garret Carter, recalled a darkly comic moment before the show. Carter said, "We were in the dressing room, and suddenly Tom ran to the window and said, 'Jane, I'm going to jump.' I grabbed him and said, 'Listen to me, Tom Williams, you'd have to go head first, because it's only one story down and you'll just break your leg.'"[7]

RESPONSE TO CRITICISM MAKES THE WRITER

Tom Williams endured his opening night. The St. Louis critics stated that *Fugitive Kind* needed revision. They called Williams's work exciting, new, vital, and colorful.

However, they felt Williams was groping for his personal style of expression. If he were to become a successful and innovative playwright, he would have to find this style and stay true to it.

Tom Williams knew he had to work harder, revise more, and master his structural problems. It did not matter what was inside his head. It mattered what he conveyed to his audience members. His characters had to express the author's story. It was *their* speeches, actions, tears, and dreams that counted.

Williams wrote his feelings about taking criticism:

> While temporarily painful, criticism of this sort proves of particular benefit to a writer in the long run, especially when his aim is toward technical improvement that may eventually enable him to say things he thinks worth saying rather than toward the enjoyment of a present success. If a writer . . . recognizes his failures and has an ideal of perfection—then the ultimate outcome may be better for those initial discouragements.[8]

Williams would always be stung by criticism. He would turn around and use it toward revision and strengthening of his work. His greatest plays would be revised many times. This ideal of perfection became so high that Williams continued revising his works until he died.

FROM TOM TO TENNESSEE

Thomas Lanier Williams did not become Tennessee Williams until after he graduated from the University of

Tennessee Williams

Iowa. He claimed that when he lived in the Alpha Tau Omega fraternity house during his senior year in Iowa City, the fellows decided he had a Southern accent. His speech sounded funny to their Midwestern ears. Although his father, Cornelius, was raised in Tennessee, Tom Williams had spent his first seven years in Mississippi and probably did reflect that Southern style of speech. He recalled that his frat brothers settled on Tennessee for his nickname. Williams was also looking for a way to stand out and be memorable. When he started to send plays to contests and agents in New York, he began to use the name Tennessee Williams. It was a name that people definitely remembered.

Maxwell Anderson, Lillian Hellman, Sidney Howard, Clifford Odets, William Saroyan, and Eugene O'Neill were Broadway playwrights of the 1930s. Tennessee Williams's dramas were different from any of their plays, unique in style and context. We do not know for sure how many of these other playwrights' works he would have read or seen. Williams would have to find his own path as a playwright and the courage to stick to it.

WILLIAMS'S AMAZING BODY OF WORK

According to most chronologies, Williams had twenty-four full-length plays produced in his lifetime. Some were not successful or enduring. Others, such as *The Glass Menagerie*, *A Streetcar Named Desire*, *The Rose Tattoo*, *Camino*

Real, Cat on a Hot Tin Roof, Garden District [Something Unspoken and *Suddenly Last Summer], Sweet Bird of Youth, The Night of the Iguana, Period of Adjustment, The Milk Train Doesn't Stop Here Anymore, Summer and Smoke,* and *Small Craft Warnings,* were widely produced, and are regularly revived today. Williams won the New York Drama Critics' Circle award four times, the Pulitzer prize twice, the Donaldson Award, the Sidney Howard Memorial Award, and the Tony Award for Best Play during his life as a playwright.

Williams wrote many one-act plays, which are usually produced in groupings. He also penned six short-story collections, two volumes of poetry, and two novels. Top screenwriters turned Williams's plays into fifteen films. Williams acted as screenwriter on seven of them. All were considered successful, and some received Academy Awards. Some of Williams's dramas returned as original film productions on television. Many talented actors played the leads in Tennessee Williams's plays on both the stage and the screen. Williams's work boosted the careers of stage and film directors, actors, and designers. The number and importance of Williams's plays rival that of any other American dramatist.

POET AS PLAYWRIGHT

Tennessee Williams often stated that he admired the poetry of D. H. Lawrence, Walt Whitman, Emily Dickinson, and especially Hart Crane. These poets were all

WRITERS OF NOTE

D. H. Lawrence (1885–1930)—British novelist and poet known for frankly exploring human need and sexual relationships.

Emily Dickinson (1830–1886)—Massachusetts author of 1,800 poems, famed for her innovative use of meter, metaphors, and subjects.

Hart Crane (1899–1932)—Ohio born poet and powerful modernist who struggled with his homosexuality within his role as a writer.

Walt Whitman (1819–1892)—New York poet-journalist known for his experimental free verse.

considered passionate, lyrical writers. The term *lyrical* poet means that the writer's stanzas are flowing and musical like a song. Lyrical poetry expresses the writer's deep personal feelings and emotions. Williams felt such an affinity to Hart Crane that he carried a copy of his works at all times. As he began to work at playwriting, Williams transferred his poetic impulses to the stage. His characters sang, as did the lyrical poet, the dilemmas of the human heart.

THE TROUBLED WILLIAMS FAMILY

The complex family of Tennessee Williams

homas Lanier Williams was born March 26, 1911, the first son of Edwina Dakin and Cornelius Williams. Tom's parents came from families of long standing in the South. Edwina Williams, a petite, attractive brunette, relocated often due to her father's career. Reverend Walter Edwin Dakin was first a teacher, then an Episcopal priest. He kept his wife and daughter on the move to better parishes and rectories. By the time she married, Edwina had lived in towns throughout Ohio, Tennessee, and Mississippi.

To record the events of her restless life, Edwina kept a diary. She wrote about her many boyfriends, known as "gentlemen callers." She also confessed to her diary that she had a "secret ambition, to become an actress, a musical comedy star."[1] The respectable Southern minister's daughter would soon give up that dream.

Edwina was living in Columbus, Mississippi, in 1906, when she performed songs from *The Mikado* for a charity show. A gentleman from Memphis, Tennessee, watched her sing and fell in love. He was Cornelius Coffin Williams, there to represent the telephone company in a court case. A veteran of the Spanish-American War, Cornelius Williams was older, tall, rugged, and determined to woo Edwina. In 1907, after dating Edwina and proposing several times, he sent an engagement ring through the mail. Edwina at age twenty-three was ready to wed. "'Many men have said I love you,' she wrote in her diary on June 1, 1907, 'but only three said Will you marry me. I will marry one next Monday. Finis. Goodbye.'"[2]

The couple lived several years in Gulfport, Mississippi, where Cornelius was a telephone company manager. Edwina, when her first baby was due, returned to the rectory in Columbus. There Rose was born in 1909. Edwina decided she might as well live with her parents rather than take the responsibility of life on her own with a baby. By 1910, Cornelius had become a traveling salesman. He returned to the habits of drinking and gambling he had enjoyed as a youth. After son Thomas was born in 1911, Edwina doted on the boy completely.

In her memoirs, Edwina recalled that although Cornelius usually visited once a month, one entire summer "I did not see my husband at all. Occasionally he would pick me up . . . and we would drive off in his car for the weekend."[3] When her father, Reverend Dakin, took a parish in Nashville, Tennessee, Edwina, Rose, and Tom followed along.

TOM'S FAMILY CIRCLE

Rose at age four and Tom at age two were cared for by a young black female servant they called Ozzie. Grandfather taught Tom to love books and literature, often "reciting passages for him from Milton, the *Iliad*, and . . . Shakespeare."[4] Tom's most beloved family member was "Grand," Edwina's mother. Tom hardly recognized Cornelius as a father. Recalling his shyness during visits, Tom said: "Often the voice of my father was jovial or boisterous. But sometimes it was harsh . . . and sounded like thunder."[5]

Edwina went out a lot socially and did welcome the excitement of Cornelius's weekend visits. At the end of 1915, Edwina's parents moved again, to the small village of Clarksdale, Mississippi, near the border south of Memphis. Apparently, Ozzie came along, as Tom fondly remembered her caring for him and telling thrilling ghost stories.

ILLNESS ALTERS TOM'S LIFE

During the summer of 1916, Tom had a terrifying experience. He was stricken with a severe case of diphtheria.

This disease, for which there were no effective drugs at the time, took the lives of many children. Edwina dropped all her church and social activities to nurse Tom. She sang to him, acted out stories, and smothered him with affection. After a painful recovery of almost two years, Tom regained the ability to walk and play.

In Tom's opinion, he had changed forever in his relationship with his mother. "My mother's overly solicitous attention planted in me the makings of a sissy, much to my father's discontent."[6] Because he had been in such frail health, Edwina discouraged rugged boyish play. During the summer of 1918, Tom was uprooted from his small town life with his grandparents. Cornelius got a steady job in the large city of St. Louis, where he moved his wife and children.

CORNELIUS'S MOVE AFFECTS ALL

The Williams family first landed in a St. Louis boardinghouse. Edwina Williams had never actually learned to cook. At age seven, Tom was teased about his Mississippi accent. He missed Grand, Grandfather, and Ozzie. Still weakened from diphtheria, he was forbidden to play on sports teams. "I preferred to play by myself," Tom recalled. "I had already stopped making connections with other boys."[7] He moved deeper into the world of books and his own imagination.

In February 1919, Tom and Rose found a baby brother,

Walter Dakin Williams, had entered the family. As a violent epidemic of Spanish influenza swept the nation, Edwina Williams contracted a case. Grand Dakin rushed up from Mississippi to care for Tom, Rose, and baby Dakin. As always, Tom was delighted to see her. "Grand was all that we knew of God in our lives!" he would later say.[8]

Cornelius Williams kept up his career as a manager at International Shoe in St. Louis. His wife's job was to keep finding roomier apartments on better streets. They moved a dozen times through Tom's youth and teen years. The children had to adjust to new neighborhoods and schools constantly.

Edwina Williams's health problems and surgeries made Tom increasingly anxious. Rose, emotionally unstable at best, grew terrified she would lose her mother. Dakin was growing up in the middle of this tumult. He admitted, "Life at home was terrible . . . by the late 1920s, mother and father were in open warfare, and both were good combatants."[9]

WRITING BECOMES TOM'S REFUGE

Tom remained slender and short in stature like his mother. His father never understood him and sometimes called him "Miss Nancy." In junior high, Tom began to express himself through writing. Working on school publications would help him relate to his fellow students.

Delighted, his mother bought him his first manual typewriter. In 1924, his first official published piece came out in his junior-high-school newspaper, *The Junior Life*. It was called "Isolated."[10]

Edwina Williams began to call Tom her writer son. This further angered Tom's father, Cornelius, who believed writers were an odd bunch that never made any money. Tom's passion for writing further alienated him from his father. One thing that Tom's father did provide were summer visits with Tom's two affectionate aunts. Isabel "Belle" Brownlow of Knoxville, Tennessee, and her sister, Ella, offered Tom needed support. Aunt Belle taught him to swim, his favorite exercise for life. Tom and Rose found a sense of freedom with their summer friends in Knoxville. Rose, a rebellious teenager of sixteen, got fourteen-year-old Tom involved in schemes with her pals.

TOM LOVES HAZEL BUT LOSES ROSE

Hazel Kramer was Tom's neighbor when they were in grade school on Taylor Street. They became best friends. Throughout high school, Tom and Hazel grew, according to Dakin, "extremely close." Often Tom made up stories, and Hazel did the illustrations. Hazel was probably as thrilled as Tom when he won his first professional story contest. His entry was a piece called "Can a Good Wife Be a Good Sport?" for *Smart Set* magazine. Hazel kept Tom's spirits up by going with him to movies, dances, and boat trips on the Mississippi.

Tom's lifelong companion, his sister, Rose, was growing strange to him. Not only was Rose obsessed with attracting boys and defying her mother, she was also drifting into a dangerous state of emotional illness. Tom remembered his feelings about Rose in a poem, "Recuerdo," published in 1952.

Some of the lines in the poem evoke character types from Williams's plays. When he says, for example, that "Love's explosion" in his schizophrenic sister, Rose, "consumingly shone in her transparent heart for a season/ And burned it out, a tissue-paper lantern,"[11] we are reminded of Blanche Dubois in *A Streetcar Named Desire* and that character's similarly fragile state.

By 1928, Rose had spent a year at school near her Aunt Ella and Aunt Belle in Knoxville. When she returned home, Tom recalled that she remained alone in her room. The only company she wanted was Tom. Symptoms of depression and irrational fears overwhelmed Rose. Tom, a busy junior at University City High School, tried to include his sister in his social activities with Hazel and their friends. He loved Rose, but could not cure her or save her.

A TRIUMPH IN PUBLISHING

By that summer, two exciting events offered Tom hope for the future. A national magazine titled *Weird Tales* printed Tom's story "The Vengeance of Nitocris" in its August

A high school yearbook portrait of Tom Williams.

issue and paid him the sum of thirty-five dollars.[12] The second event was the chance to absorb European culture on a church tour led by his grandfather, Reverend Walter Dakin. Tom's passion for travel probably began during this rambling trip.

As a senior, Tom wrote for the school paper and produced travel articles. Tom convinced his father to send him to the University of Missouri to major in journalism. He passed his senior finals, then forgot to tell his mother when his graduation ceremony would take place. In fact he forgot to attend himself. This absentminded behavior was becoming a bad habit with Tom. His mind was always on the next piece he was writing.

OFF TO "MIZZOU"

Tom's college career began with his mother accompanying him to the campus at Columbia, Missouri, on the train. In a letter to Grandfather, Tom wrote: "Mother . . . acts as though I were leaving for war instead of college."[13] To placate his father, Tom pledged a fraternity, Alpha Tau Omega (ATO). It was required that every male student enroll in the Reserve Officers' Training Corps (ROTC) as well. Suddenly, between his courses and his fraternity life, Tom found himself in the company of many young men. This was a change from his life in junior high and high school, where he socialized mostly with his sister and his girlfriends.

Tom learned to function at get-togethers at the fraternity.

His ATO friend Elmer Lower recalled: "He had a quietly ironic wit. . . . His small monthly allowance came from his father, and at mail call Tom held up the check and announced, 'The Red Goose flies again!'"[14] Red Goose shoes were produced by Cornelius Williams's branch of International Shoe.

At the University of Missouri, Tom began to write one-act plays along with his poems and stories. Throughout his college years, he wrote constantly and entered every contest he could find. His grades were usually Bs and Cs in his courses. However, he was becoming more absorbed with drama. He studied the plays of Norwegian Henrik Ibsen and Swede August Strindberg. These playwrights' characters suffered from troubled human relationships. Ibsen and Strindberg used symbols in their plays and searched for moral truth. They explored the dark and complex influence of the parent upon the child, certainly an interest of Tom's.

IRONY—*The incongruity of an expected situation (or its outcome) and the actual situation (or its outcome). In language, irony is the deliberate use of words to contrast an apparent meaning with the words' intended meaning (which are usually the complete opposite of each other).*

HENRIK IBSEN (1828–1906)—*Norwegian playwright responsible for the rise of modern realistic drama.*

AUGUST STRINDBERG (1849–1912)—*Swedish playwright, novelist, and story writer whose dark, radical treatment of marriage, sexual affairs, and family relationships made him infamous.*

Elmer Lower stated that "there was absolutely no indication that Tom would become America's greatest playwright . . . he was unremarkable in every way."[15] Unfortunately, he was most unremarkable in his grades. After forgetting to attend exams, neglecting to turn in papers, and refusing to do his ROTC duty, Tom's college grade average was on the low end. His angry father kept him home after 1932, refusing to send him back for his senior year.

HARD TIMES SEND TOM WILLIAMS TO WORK

In 1933, Tom Williams was forced to work for the International Shoe Company. He had already worked there throughout the summer of 1931 as a clerk. The economic depression had caused his father to insist his son help pay his way. Rose, unable to hold a job or find a husband, became a drain on her father. Her terrible relationship with him got even worse. Her brother felt sad and protective of her. Rose eventually had stays in sanatoriums and hospital wards for psychiatric treatment.

One special event happened to Tom Williams in 1934 that impacted on his future life. He saw a performance at a St. Louis theater of *Ghosts* by Henrik Ibsen. The powerful acting amazed him. The forbidden subject matter of inherited venereal disease astounded him. He stated that it was "one of the things that made me want to write for the theatre."[16]

Tom Williams was a poor worker for International Shoe. His lack of focus caused him to lose orders. He stayed up nights drinking coffee, reading, and writing. Stress over his writing career, and hidden anxiety about his uncertain sexual orientation, took its toll. In early 1935, he had something he called a "cardiac seizure." He said that a doctor told him that "I did indeed have a defective heart."[17]

Perhaps Tom Williams's heart had been weakened by virulent diphtheria. His poor eating and sleeping habits, dependence on caffeine and nicotine, combined with stress, could set off a seizure. He was underweight, exhausted, and seriously depressed.

Cornelius Williams faced the fact that his older son was a failure in the business world. He allowed him to resign on his twenty-fourth birthday, March 11, 1935, and recuperate at his grandparents' home in their parish in Memphis. There Tom Williams saw the first production of one of his plays, a one-act called *Cairo! Shanghai! Bombay!* The audience applauded this light comedy. He wrote later: "Then and there the theatre and I found each other for better and for worse. I know it's the only thing that saved my life."[18]

A PLAYWRIGHT EMERGES

Living back with his parents in St. Louis, Tom Williams enrolled at nearby Washington University and wrote constantly. The school year went poorly for him, and he did not pass the year with enough credits to graduate. However, he was able to attend more productions at the American Theatre, where he sat in the cheapest balcony seats. He soon discovered the Mummers of St. Louis, a community theater. They liked his first full play, *Candles to the Sun*. Their production of it gave him the confidence he needed to transfer his credits and enroll in the University of Iowa, a school well known for its theater program. In the fall of 1937, Williams headed for Iowa City.

He learned a great deal during his year in the University of Iowa's theater department, both about playwriting and about producing plays in general. While living in the ATO fraternity house, he kept a journal from which this self-assessment tells how hard he was trying to understand himself. Admitting he was homesick, missed Jiggs, his terrier, and was neglecting his studies and his writing, Williams listed his "virtues—I am kind, friendly, modest, sympathetic, tolerant, and sensitive." Then he listed his "faults—I am ego-centric, introspective, morbid, sensual, irreligious, lazy, timid, and cowardly."[19] He closed by insisting he did have "guts of a sort," even though he was a "stinking sissy." That Williams would integrate these accurately described "faults" and "virtues" into a gifted, productive playwright was hard at the time to believe.

The chairman of the Iowa theater department did not think the plays Williams wrote for him, *Spring Storm* and *Not About Nightingales*, showed much talent. He rejected Williams's request to return for another year on a fellowship.

Although Tom Williams finished his college degree in August 1938 at age twenty-seven, he was not equipped to earn a living at anything but writing.

He tried to get a job on a Works Progress Administration (WPA) project. The WPA was the name of a group of government agencies set up to give employment to the nation's 10 million unemployed, beginning in 1935. One of the WPA's agencies was called the Federal Writers' Project and another one was the Federal Theatre Project. The WPA had an office located in New Orleans, where Williams tried to get work. In 1938, he found the city's French Quarter was filled with bars, brothels, artists, and musicians. "I've never known anybody who lived in . . . the Quarter who wasn't slightly intoxicated— without booze," Tom observed.[20] New Orleans was his kind of town.

AN ITINERANT LIFESTYLE

Tom Williams's practice of observing and absorbing peoples' lives and conversations had begun in his youth. In New Orleans, he inhaled the culture eagerly. The sexual freedom of the French Quarter allowed him to face his growing feelings of homosexuality. Here he would send out his first plays using the nickname he got from his University of Iowa pals—Tennessee. Since the WPA job never came through, he lived on scraps, part-time jobs with restaurants, and handouts from his family. He set up his lifelong plan of rising early, writing steadily through most of the day, and, after a swim (if possible), partying through the evening.

The road Tennessee Williams traveled from starving writer in New Orleans in 1939 to nationally recognized playwright was a tumultuous one. In early 1939, Williams won his first prize from the Group Theatre in New York—one hundred dollars for three one-act plays. This prize attracted a fine theatrical agent, Audrey Wood, who reviewed Williams's work and saw a special talent. Wood helped him apply for a further grant. The Dramatist Guild, through a grant from the Rockefeller Foundation, awarded him a writing fellowship of one thousand dollars by the end of 1939.[21] Although the funds kept him going as he moved from town to town, Williams was still sad. After visiting his severely mentally disturbed sister, Rose, at a Missouri mental hospital, he confessed to his journal that he felt guilty he could not share even a bit of this blessing with her. He called her beyond the reach of joy.

GROUP THEATRE— *Formed in 1931 in New York, this company held left-wing political views and produced plays that explored social issues.*

DRAMATIST GUILD OF AMERICA—*Organization that for 100 years has promoted and protected professional interests of playwrights, composers, lyricists, and librettists.*

ENTERING THE PROFESSIONAL THEATER

Battle of Angels, Williams's first full professional production, was produced by the Theatre Guild in Boston from December 20, 1940 to January 11, 1941. The play's ambience was similar to the close-knit village of Clarksdale, Mississippi, where Williams had spent his early childhood years. The story of the handsome drifter Val and his potent, erotic effect on the married storekeeper Myra, the wealthy, alcoholic Sandra, the artistic Vee, and other townswomen was boldly, poetically told. The characters and plot had many underlying references to both the New Testament story of Christ, and the Greek myth of Odysseus. The Boston critics were offended and negative about its innovative dramatic effects. To Williams's dismay, the play failed.

THEATRE GUILD— *Founded in 1919 in New York, this producing group was owned by its board of directors, which included playwrights, actors, and designers. It was noted for giving new authors a chance to develop. Some younger radical members broke away and formed the Group Theatre.*

During the period of 1942 to 1943, Tennessee Williams was broke again. He begged for rooms and meals from friends, moving from city to city, beach to beach. He was forced to return to his parents at times if only to take a bath and sleep in a bed. In 1943, Williams was on the road, heading for a Hollywood studio that hired him to do screen writing. In January, his mother wrote him that his sister, Rose, a difficult, often violent patient at a state mental hospital for six years, had a prefrontal lobotomy. This radical brain surgery frightened Williams, but he could do nothing about Rose at that time. He needed the Hollywood job, mainly for the money. No matter how much the studio paid, Williams found he could not write anything except what came from his heart.

Agent Audrey Wood understood Tennessee Williams well. Without Wood, Williams might never have had the career he did. Wood even took care of such personal matters as his draft classification card. She wrote to him in 1942: "I'm keeping the original because if I sent it to you, you might lose it."[22] Williams was classified 4F. This meant his physical problems with his bad eyesight and heart kept him from being drafted for combat in World War II.

A long awaited miracle arrived for Williams late in 1944. During 1940, he wrote a draft of a play called *Stairs to the Roof*. It partly concerned a young aspiring poet stuck working in a shoe factory. Williams took elements of this play, then added the writer's mother and sister to the plot. Incorporating additional material from some of his short stories, Williams named this new play *The Gentleman Caller*. He tried to sell it to the Hollywood studio as a screenplay, but failed. Again he reworked it as a stage play, now calling it *The Glass Menagerie*. This version struck gold with a professional New York producer. Revolutionary in style, concept, and structure, this play would make Tennessee Williams famous and financially secure.

A NEW STYLE OF DRAMA

Examining *The Glass Menagerie*

The first production of *The Glass Menagerie* opened in Chicago on December 26, 1944. Tennessee Williams said, "No one knew how to take *Menagerie*, it was something of an innovation in the theatre."[1] The play was different from most realistic American dramas of the 1930s and early 1940s. In fact, it was different from Williams's first major plays, *Fugitive Kind* and *Battle of Angels*. It lacked their sharpness and social commentary. It had little sexual interchange and no violence. In 1965, the author told *The New York Times* that on his last typed version of this play, he wrote: "*The Glass Menagerie*, a rather dull little play by Tennessee Williams."[2]

The play's action was simple. A middle-aged mother, deserted by her husband, is dependent on her restless adult son and devoted to her reclusive adult daughter. Her goal is to keep the family together financially and emotionally during hard times. The son's goal is to break his ties to his mother and sister and seek adventure in the world. The action takes place in the Wingfields' cramped St. Louis apartment and on its fire escape. Dynamic plot development and resolution were never Williams's primary concerns in writing this play.

This story, partly drawn from Williams's short story called "Portrait of a Girl in Glass," is a nostalgic, painful series of memories in which the narrator recreates his family. These characters' moods and feelings are more important than a well-constructed plot. Emotional journeys take precedence over physical action. *The Glass Menagerie* would become a play about the love, frustration, compassion, and human weakness that all families experience.

THE MEANING OF TIME AND REALITY

In *Glass Menagerie*, Tom Wingfield, the adult son, is also the narrator of the play. He says he is giving us "truth in the pleasant disguise of illusion." This lets us know that the truth may be painful. Tom Wingfield explains that the play is taking place in his memory. Happenings may not be presented realistically because memory is seated in the heart.

We do not know how many years have passed between the "present" of Tom the narrator and the "past" of the family's life together. The characters and incidents are crystallized, captured in the moments they shared.

For each character, *time* has a different meaning. For the *Son*, time has been stalled. All he wants is to break free and get into forward motion. For the *Daughter*, time is slowly creeping. She would like to stop time altogether and live in the fragile, frozen world of her glass collection. For the *Mother*, time has already passed. All she can do is cling to her control of the family and remember. Her chance to have a comfortable, loving relationship with a man seems over. For the *Gentleman Caller*, time is roaring ahead. He grabs on to its tail and rushes into the world of the future.

Williams blends all four characters and their different perceptions into a single frame. He wrote his ideas about the nature of time and reality while working on this play. "The only reality . . . that has form and dimension is the one that exists in recollection. Now is formless, now is almost breathless, now is something too little even to measure."[3] Williams means that we can only really know something that has already passed. The present is too fast to capture or reflect upon. However, he does allow his characters to have their own reality, as they share hurts and disappointments in their time together.

THE CHARACTERS SEEM FAMILIAR

By the time *The Glass Menagerie* opened, Williams was thirty-three years old. He had been writing steadily since he was a teenager. Sometimes he preferred to go hungry and homeless rather than take a meaningless day job. He said he was "a compulsive typist and a compulsive writer

. . . that's my life . . . my intense life is my work."[4] One of the few jobs he was forced to take to survive was in the offices and warehouse of the International Shoe Company.

Tom Wingfield, the Son in *Menagerie*, is also forced to work at the local shoe company. He escapes by writing poetry on shoe boxes and going to the movies. Tom Wingfield loves his sister but cannot really help her. He respects his mother but cannot stand daily life with her. Desperate for travel and adventure to feed his creativity, he is much like the author Tom Williams. However, there was an important difference in Williams's life. In the play, the Father has taken off years before, giving the Son a model of escape. Williams had to contend with his real father. Cornelius Williams did live at home and support the family. He fought often with his wife, openly disliked his older son, Tom, and disapproved of his daughter.

Laura Wingfield suffers from a slight physical disability that causes her to limp. Her nervous, shy, introverted personality made her a failure in school. Laura's ability to hold a business position or attract a husband fades as she moves into a private world. Tom Williams, during the years he lived at home after college, recalled his sister's white room with its shelves of miniature glass animals as a refuge. Williams said in an interview: "[H]er glass menagerie had a meaning for me. The glass animals came to represent the fragile, delicate ties that must be broken . . . when you try to fulfill yourself."[5]

Rose Williams had a different set of problems than Laura Wingfield has. Her lively good looks often attracted men. However, her overwrought personality and emotional imbalance kept her suitors from proposing marriage. Rose's actual mental illness was not diagnosed in the 1930s. Rose was also too nervous to work in business. Unlike Laura, Rose was discontent and became increasingly violent. Her darkening mental condition forced her into institutions.

Amanda Wingfield may be the character closest to her Williams family counterpart. Amanda's life centers on running her home and her children's lives. She can be demanding and dramatic and a frantically lively talker. She is proud to be an officer in the St. Louis Daughters of the American Revolution. She is clever at economizing. Memories of her youth filled with parties and suitors in her Mississippi community are recounted to her children. When we meet her in her late forties, Amanda is clinging to a charm that is fading like the Old South. In these ways, she is a reflection of Edwina Dakin Williams.

A major break in reality between Amanda Wingfield and Edwina Williams occurs when Tennessee Williams removes the husband/father figure from the home. Mr. Wingfield's desertion deeply affects Amanda, Laura, and Tom. All Father leaves behind is a large smiling portrait. When Tom explodes at Amanda for taking away his books by D. H. Lawrence (the British novelist and poet whom Williams said he idolized), he tells her: "If self is what I thought of, Mother, I'd be where he is—GONE! [He points to his father's picture.] As far as the system of transportation reaches!"[6]

44

Edwina Williams's husband, Cornelius, was all too present. They fought over many issues, but he did pay the bills. Edwina did not work outside the household, even during hard times. Tom Williams, however, believed that in one way his father was absent. Cornelius never made him feel that he loved any of them except young Dakin. In his twenties, Tom Williams said that he felt he was important only to his father "because I was the namesake of his own father, Thomas Lanier Williams II."[7] Tom Williams was shy of his father and uncomfortable when alone with him.

In its earlier versions, *The Glass Menagerie* was called *The Caller* or *The Gentleman Caller*. This may seem strange,

Tennessee Williams in his twenties with his younger brother Dakin Williams.

since the character of the Gentleman Caller, named Jim O'Connor, is an outsider. The Gentleman Caller was very important to the author, however. He portrayed the average ambitious workingman. Tom says of Jim that he is the emissary from the world of reality, a place from which the Wingfield family is set apart. Jim has never been the poet or the dreamer. He is the popular fellow Laura adored from afar in high school. Amanda sees him as representing the future American. She hopes he is a link to a prosperous life for Laura. Tom Wingfield says that "like some archetype of the universal unconscious, the image of the gentleman caller haunted our small apartment . . . ."[8]

As the play ends, the only character with a defined, achievable goal outside his present situation is Jim O'Connor. He has already found a girl to marry, a fact that Tom never realized when he brought him to dinner. Amanda and Laura are totally unprepared to succeed in the postwar half of the twentieth century. Tom's goal is to escape the corporate grind. He takes the money needed to pay the electric bill and uses it to join the Merchant Marine. Trying to break his attachment to his sister, Tom says he "followed, from then on, in my father's footsteps, attempting to find in motion what was lost in space."[9]

CHILDHOOD AND FAMILY PRESSURES

Williams continued to study the effect of childhood trauma on his adult characters. In the Wingfield family, each character is shaped by loss. Amanda has lost the romantic possibilities of marrying well and living the pampered life she was raised to expect. She chose to marry a charming but irresponsible man. His desertion has cost her dearly. Amanda's family gave her no realistic way to support herself.

Laura tries to be the girl her mother needs at home. When out in the world, she is a solitary loner. Laura deeply loves her brother and mother, and tries to keep the peace between them. She cannot meet their needs and expectations. Jim the Gentleman Caller said to her regarding their high-school days: "[Y]ou had this inferiority complex that keeps you from feeling comfortable with people. Somebody needs to build your confidence up and make you proud instead of shy and turning away . . . "[10]

Tom is the most obviously affected by family stress. He cannot replace his runaway father, nor can he stand his mother's nagging and suspicions. Claiming his enemies plan to dynamite their apartment, Tom shouts: "You'll go up, up on a broomstick, over Blue Mountain with seventeen gentlemen callers! You ugly—babbling old—witch!"[11] Later as he apologizes, Tom tells Amanda she cannot know what is inside his heart.

Loneliness and Limitations as Themes

In a 1948 interview, Tennessee Williams said: "For me the dominating premise has been the need for understanding and tenderness and fortitude among individuals trapped by circumstances."[12] In other interviews, Williams discussed human loneliness as being a major theme in his writing.

All of the Wingfields are trapped by circumstance and unfulfilled need. The emotional climax of the play, states Professor Roger Boxill, is when Tom recognizes that "for all the miles he has traveled he has never really broken the tender ties with his mother and his sister."[13] Although Tom departed in anger, with his mother calling him a "selfish dreamer" and his sister retreating into her world of glass figures, he is still connected to them.

Tom Wingfield tells us about the last contact the family had from their fleeing father. It is a postcard that reads: "Hello—Goodbye!" This sets up a theme about life's anticipations and ultimately life's limits and loss. Scholar Judith Thompson writes that the pattern of this play is seen when one compares Amanda's wild success as a belle with many callers to Laura's one futile evening with Jim O'Connor. The play's pattern becomes "the inevitable fall of romantic aspirations to existential limitations."[14] This means that life's realities must always limit our dreams.

POETIC IMAGERY IN DIALOGUE

Some critics think that the image of the Wingfields goes beyond that of a struggling single mother, a reclusive daughter, and a dreamer escapist son. Judith Thompson

Karen Allen and John Malkovich star as Laura and Tom Wingfield in the 1987 film adaptation of *The Glass Menagerie*, directed by Paul Newman.

sees the image of this family as universal. They represent modern man's separation from God and his fellow human beings. She believes Williams uses poetic imagery in an otherwise realistic drama to make this metaphor clear.

Examples of poetic images are:

Amanda: You did all this to deceive me, just for deception?
Laura: Mother, when you're disappointed, you get that awful suffering look on your face, like the picture of Jesus' mother in the museum!

Amanda: I've seen such pitiful cases in the South—barely tolerated spinsters living upon the grudging patronage of sister's husband or brother's wife—stuck away in some little mousetrap of a room—encouraged by one in-law to visit another—little birdlike women without any nest—eating the crust of humility all their life!

Tom: Man is by instinct a lover, a hunter, a fighter, and none of those instincts are give much play at the warehouse!

Tom: [about the Paradise Dance Hall] . . . a large glass sphere that hung from the ceiling. It would turn slowly about and filter the dusk with delicate rainbow colors . . . Couples would come outside . . . you could see them kissing behind ash pits and telephone poles. This was the compensation for lives that passed like mine, without any change or adventure. . . . All the world was waiting for bombardments.

Amanda: [about her girlhood] So lovely, that country

in May, all lacy with dogwood, literally flooded with jonquils. . . . It was a joke, Amanda and her jonquils. No vases to hold them? All right, I'll hold them myself. And then I—met your father. Malaria fever and jonquils and then—this—boy . . .

Tom: [as the Narrator] The cities swept about me like dead leaves, leaves that were brightly colored but torn away from the branches. . . . I pass the lighted window of a shop where perfume is sold. The window is filled with pieces of colored glass, tiny transparent bottles in delicate colors, like bits of a shattered rainbow. Then all at once my sister touches my shoulder . . . Oh, Laura, Laura, I tried to leave you behind me, but I am more faithful than I intended to be!

Tennessee Williams's theater speech draws on the natural rhythm and imagery he absorbed as a boy in Mississippi. He uses such devices as music, visual images projected onto screens, and special unreal lighting effects to bring his meaning to the stage.

SYMBOLS MAKE THE PLAY RICHER

Wishing on the moon over the delicatessen symbolizes Amanda's belief in her child's romantic future, in spite of the poor mundane life they lead. The candles and candelabra Laura uses to light her scenes are religious symbols. They came from an old church altar, and make Laura seem soft, virginal, almost angelic. Laura's glass unicorn, accidentally broken by Jim, comes from folklore. We do not know if Williams knew that the single horn of the unicorn in medieval legend was said to heal people from poison—or if he simply saw a unicorn in his sister Rose's glass collection. When Laura's unicorn horn is broken off, we see that this reflects a special creature (like Laura) attempting to become like everyone else, which will never happen. Amanda Wingfield herself is a symbol of the lost culture of the Old South. Jim O'Connor is a symbol of the modern capitalist culture of 1945.

CRITICS DISAGREED ON MEANING

Critics at the New York opening did not all understand or agree on what *The Glass Menagerie* characters meant. Robert Garland, *New York Journal-American*, February 4, 1945, wrote: "The Mother might as well be known as Fallen Grandeur. . . . Her Daughter, an unhappy moon-like cripple." Ward Morehouse, *New York Sun*, February 4, 1945, wrote: "Her daughter is the psychopathic Laura, who lives in a dream world . . . Amanda is bitter, pitiful, and ridiculous . . . " Burton Rascoe, *New York World-Telegram*, February 4, 1945, wrote:

> She was there—a simple, sanely insane, horrible
> Mother, pathetic and terribly human and terribly
> real. She succeeded in destroying every vestige of
> hope and beauty and joy in the lives of the two
> people who loved her—her son and daughter . . . she
> is a fluttery hen with her two soul-misshapen brood

. . . she doesn't even love her son, she merely keeps him under a sense of obligation.

In spite of their diverse opinions, the critics generally agreed with Garland, when he wrote: "[T]he playwriting, which is memorable; the playacting, which is flawless; and the production, which is inimitable—makes 'The Glass Menagerie' a masterpiece of make-believe."[15]

The Glass Menagerie won the New York Drama Critics Circle award for the best play of 1945, as well as several other monetary awards. It was a big commercial success. Tennessee Williams would sign contracts with producers and publishers. He granted half his royalties from this play to his mother, Edwina Dakin Williams, for the rest of her life.

NEW YORK DRAMA CRITICS CIRCLE— *Theater critics from all the New York City newspapers and magazines except for the* New York Times, *who vote on the Best Play, Best Musical, and Best Foreign Play each year on Broadway.*

DARK DESIRE

Examining *A Streetcar Named Desire*

From his poorer days in 1938 through his new prosperity, Tennessee Williams often retreated to New Orleans. Although *The Glass Menagerie* made Williams a well-known success, people in New Orleans did not single him out. Artists and writers were common there. Williams also spent time in Mexico and Key West, Florida. Wherever he moved, he took his portable typewriter and trunks of manuscripts along.

During the winter of 1946, when Williams lived on Orleans Street in New Orleans, his mind was bursting with projects. He worked on a one-act play he called *Ten Blocks on the Camino Real*, which would evolve until it became a full-length production in 1953. He had begun a play that would be called *Summer and Smoke*. Another story had been percolating in his mind during the run of *Menagerie* in New York. It involved what he called a contest between the crude sensibilities of working-class poker players and the delicacies of two Southern women.[1]

Although Cornelius Williams regularly played poker in St. Louis hotels, his older son, Tom, had never played the game. So Tennessee Williams invited men from the

Broadway crew of *Menagerie* to come to his New York hotel suite and play poker. To the crew's surprise, Williams took notes on all they said and did. These poker lessons helped shape the characters of his new play, *A Poker Night*. He continued work on it in New Orleans, naming it *A Streetcar Named Desire*, for the car that ran past his apartment.

PERSONAL RELATIONS INFLUENCE THE PLAY

Williams worked on this play, along with other short stories and plays, through 1946 and into 1947. In Williams's personal life, changes occurred. Although in his mid-thirties, Tennessee Williams had never had a long-term love relationship. During this period, a younger man named Pancho Rodriguez Gonzalez moved in with Williams. The pair moved back and forth between New Orleans and New York and summered on Nantucket Island. They were joined for the winter of 1947 in New Orleans by Reverend Walter Dakin, Williams's elderly grandfather.

Tennessee Williams and Pancho Gonzalez began as a good balance. Williams said of Pancho, "He relieved me of my greatest affliction, which is perhaps the major theme of my writings, the affliction of loneliness."[2] Yet Tennessee Williams was not able to break his long habit of casual sexual affairs. Gonzalez was determined that they be faithful and committed. They fought often, sometimes physically. During this tumultuous relationship with

Gonzalez, Tennessee Williams completed *A Streetcar Named Desire*.

The play opened on Broadway in December 1947 after Williams had personally auditioned Jessica Tandy in Hollywood to play Blanche. As for casting Stanley, director Elia Kazan recommended a young stage actor named Marlon Brando. Williams recalled that Brando drove up to Williams's rental cottage on Cape Cod. He fixed the fuses and repaired the plumbing. Brando then read for him and his director-friend Margo Jones of Dallas. Jones shouted: "This is the greatest reading I've ever heard—in or outside Texas!"[3] Brando was cast as Stanley and was forever identified with the role.

PLOT AND CHARACTER IN *STREETCAR*

The plot concerns the relationship between two sisters, the younger sister's husband, and the husband's best friend. What occurs between these four people is determined by who they were and what they did *before* the play begins. This is called prehistory.

The elder sister, Blanche, just over thirty, tells us gradually of her past misdeeds. The younger sister, Stella, about age twenty-five, has lived away from their Mississippi plantation home for many years. Much of Blanche's decline has been kept secret from Stella and Stanley. When Blanche shows up uninvited to live in Stella's small New Orleans apartment, she reveals that the last members of their family have died. The plantation home has been lost to debtors, leaving Blanche homeless. Gradually we discover that Blanche has lost her job teaching high-school English. Due to her affairs with various men in their hometown, Blanche is no longer welcome in the community.

Stella's prehistory is simpler. Ten years ago, the summer her father died, Stella left the family home and moved to New Orleans to find a job. She met and married Stanley Kowalski and became a housewife. In the course of the play, she also becomes a mother.

Stanley's prehistory is that he was, as Stella states, "A master sergeant in the Engineers' Corps." Since the play opened in December 1947, we can assume that Stanley served during part of World War II. Now a salesman of machinery, witty and shrewd, Stanley's competitive nature is seen as he plays poker with male friends. He can be violent when drunk, crude and domineering. Still, Stanley demonstrates a passionate devotion to Stella and the child she will bear.

Harold "Mitch" Mitchell's prehistory is that he is Stan's best friend, coworker at the company, and fellow veteran. He also has a history of being a caregiver to his sick mother. Stella likes and respects him and feels he might be a prospective husband for Blanche. Although Mitch is more sensitive, he is also a hard, demanding man when it comes to purity in a woman.

Stella Becomes the Pivotal Character

The plot of *Streetcar* turns on Stella. She is manipulated back and forth between her sister's demands that she leave what Blanche terms her brutish husband and her husband's growing fury that Blanche is ruining their tightly balanced marriage. A loving sister, Stella tries to find a solution for Blanche's desperate position. Yet she cannot give up her sexual fulfillment with Stanley. He is also the father and supporter of her baby. It is Stella's decision *not* to believe that Stanley has forced himself on Blanche that allows the play to end as it does.

Sexual Attraction, Fascinating Females

Scholar Louise Blackwell studied the "predicament of women" in Williams's plays. She claims all his major females "suffer from physical or emotional mutilation."[4] In the 1940s, authors rarely wrote honestly about the abuse women sometimes suffered in relationships. In the case of *Streetcar*, Blackwell notes that Blanche's prehistory includes a family of degenerates. The DuBoises gave Blanche high-class airs, culture, and education. Still, they were weaklings who wasted her land and passed on no moral strength. The Kowalskis learned how to fight for survival. They were Polish immigrants who endured hard times. They produced dominant males like Stanley. When

Vivien Leigh and Marlon Brando in the 1951 film production of *A Streetcar Named Desire*. The film was directed by Elia Kazan, who also directed the original stage production.

Stanley's masculine power collides with Blanche's sexual past and superior attitude, an explosion is bound to occur. Blanche's downfall is inevitable.

SYMBOLS AND IMAGERY DEEPEN THE TEXT

Critics have said that Blanche can be a symbol for many things. Chris Jones, writing for the *Roundabout Theatre Company Magazine*, said: "Blanche . . . is a metaphor for lost souls . . . and a reminder that so-called social progress almost always has its victims."[5] Edward Hall, director of a recent New York production, said Blanche was the kind of genteel, emotionally damaged woman that had no place in postwar America. "She's quite literally at the end of the line right from when we first meet her."[6]

Stanley may be a metaphor for the new middle-class, self-made workingman. Blanche, however, calls him an animal in Scene 4: "There's even something sub-human —something not quite to the stage of humanity yet. Yes, something ape-like about him."[7] She begs Stella to leave him and not hang back with the brutes. Stella, refusing to see this image of her husband, embraces him as soon as he returns. Later, Blanche tells Mitch, "The first time I laid eyes on him, I thought to myself, that man is my executioner. That man will destroy me."[8]

Blanche does things that symbolize how she truly sees herself. She obsessively bathes. This is because she knows that she is not clean or pure inside. Blanche keeps the lights low with colored paper lanterns on them. This allows her to keep up an illusion of youthful beauty. She tells Stella: "When people are soft—soft people have got to shimmer and glow—they've got to put on soft colors, the colors of butterfly wings, and put a—a paper lantern over the light. . . . I'm fading now. I don't know how much longer I can turn the trick."[9]

The image of the fading butterfly, flittering and falling, gives us a preview of how Blanche will fail at the end of the play.

Williams uses the poker game as a metaphor to reflect life in the Kowalski apartment. Judith Thompson writes of the game: "Stanley's fluctuating fortunes at cards reflect his changing status in the existential game of survival played between him and Blanche."[10] Stanley, a fierce card player and bitter loser, finally figures out what the real cards are in Blanche's hand. Although Blanche almost finds her savior in fellow player Mitch, Stanley makes sure she is out of the game and out of his life forever.

In Scene 8 of the play, Blanche uses candles and their light as a metaphor for purity and inner beauty. When Mitch deserts her birthday party, she asks Stella to save the candles for her baby's birthdays: "I hope the candles are going to glow in his life and I hope that his eyes are going to be like candles, like two blue candles lighted in a white cake!"[11] This echoes a similar metaphor of Laura's candles in *Glass Menagerie*.

CINEMA STYLE IN A STAGE PLAY

Just as he did in *The Glass Menagerie*, Tennessee Williams wrote directions for the staging, sets, lighting, and musical background of this play. The eleven scenes are like scenes in a film, with sudden starts of the action and dynamic conclusions. Exact lighting and sound effects, including a lot of musical underscoring, make *Streetcar* a total experience for the audience. The sounds of blues and jazz, which fill the real French Quarter in New Orleans, help create the sensuality of the play.

Low, moody lights in the apartment, ominous flashes of lightning, the moment when Mitch rips off a colored paper lantern and holds Blanche's face under the naked bulb are examples of cinematic style. These are ways to focus our vision on characters and force our response. This is what camera shots and lights do in a film.

SOCIAL STATEMENT ABOUT WOMEN'S RIGHTS

Williams stopped writing about broad socialist issues as he did in his first plays. However, he was the first playwright on the American stage to deal openly with the crime of sexual assault. Of course, the act is only hinted at as Stanley forces Blanche onto his bed and the lights go out. Yet, it was a shocking moment to see on stage. Critic Kimball King notes that although Blanche has had many sexual affairs, Stanley's assault of her is "nonetheless a rape, a crime of violence rather than simply a sexual act; we witness Blanche DuBois's destruction by Kowalski."[12]

STREETCAR GIVES THE CRITICS A RIDE

On its Broadway opening, December 4, 1947, critic Ward Morehouse wrote for the *New York Sun*: "*A Streetcar Named Desire* is not a play for the squeamish. It is often coarse and harrowing . . . but it is a playwriting job of enormous gusto and vitality and poignance."

Williams Hawkins wrote for the *New York World-Telegram*: "Williams models out of the rawest materials and his finished art is harsh realism. It is lost souls that preoccupy him." Hawkins recognizes that the play is an account of the conflict between Blanche and Stanley: "[T]he one thing they know in common is physical desire." Stanley, open and honest, likes to eat and drink and make love whenever he wants. Blanche must rationalize everything she does. Hawkins sees "the two essential planes of the character" in Blanche—and notes "There are scenes of violence and raw emotion that leave you gasping."

Louis Kronenberger wrote in *New York PM* that the play is the best of the season, "the one that reveals the most talent, the one that attempts the most truth." He sees Blanche as a "demonically driven kind of liar—the one who lies to the world because she must lie to herself."

Kronenberger said the middle of the play was too static and repetitious, but the final third with its genuine release of emotional excitement, with the conflict between Blanche and Stanley, "is quite often good drama!"[13]

The play's finale is as moving as any scene in contemporary theater. Stanley has Blanche committed to a mental institution. When the institution's doctor and matron come for Blanche, both Stella and Mitch break down in tears of guilt and regret. To keep leading their lives, Stella as Stanley's wife and mother of his child, and Mitch as Stanley's best friend, they must step aside and let Stanley get rid of Blanche. At the final moment, we can only hope that treatment will give Blanche some kind of future. As Blanche clings to the doctor, she exits, saying: "Whoever you are—I have always depended on the kindness of strangers."

WILLIAMS' PERSONAL LIFE SETTLES DOWN

Life with Williams involved his constant writing, traveling, drinking, cigarette smoking, and strange friendships. Williams, although basically a strong man, had some health issues. He had many surgeries on reoccurring cataracts on his eyes, plus intestinal problems. Anyone who lived with Tennessee Williams would have to understand his high-strung nerves and obsession with illness. He found such a man in 1948, ten years his junior. He was a Sicilian American from New Jersey named Frank Merlo.

Williams wrote about it in his *Memoirs*, saying that "it was clear to me that my heart, too long accustomed to transitory attachments, had found in the young Sicilian a home at last."[14]

Dakin Williams, knowing that his brother could always be drawn to dangerous casual sex, called Frank the best person ever in his life. "My brother left every practical detail of his life to Frank, and he discharged everything wonderfully well. He cared for Grandfather . . . Frank was a unique man."[15] Close friends Paul Bigelow and Christopher Isherwood stated that Frank Merlo was a good man who gave order to Williams's chaotic life. Maria Britneva St. Just, a young Russian actress and dancer who became Williams's great friend, said after meeting Frank in 1948 that he truly loved Tennessee Williams for what he was. "He had great integrity and great dignity."[16]

Tennessee Williams's parents and siblings had moved on with their lives as well. With the financial security Edwina Williams had from her gift of theater royalties, she was able to divorce her husband and live on her own in St. Louis. Rose Williams spent most of her time in a state mental institution in Farmington, Missouri. Dakin Williams, now a lawyer, drew up a trust for Rose. It gave her half the royalties from her brother's play *Summer and Smoke*, which opened on Broadway in 1948. This permitted her to pay for superior mental health care.

Williams's restless nature drove him, along with Frank, and sometimes with author friends Gore Vidal and Truman Capote, to tour Europe throughout 1949 and 1950.

That winter, with Frank and Grandfather Dakin in Key West, Tennessee Williams produced the first draft of *The Rose Tattoo*. He dedicated the play to Merlo, whose Sicilian family inspired it.

Biographer Ronald Hayman notes that from this time period on, Williams took up a dangerous habit. He had started "experimenting with pills—phenobarbital and secobarbital" in 1949.[17] Williams wrote to a longtime friend from New York, Donald Windham, about his life in Key West in December 1949: "[M]y ratio of concerns is something like this: 50% work and worry over work, 35% the perpetual struggle against lunacy . . . 15% a very true and very tender love for those who have been and are close to me as friends and as lover."[18] At the time, his obsession with work was growing to 89 percent. His anxiety and fear of illness was just as high as ever.

In the early 1950s, Williams combined alcohol with regular use of pills, primarily to sleep. Friends noted that he sometimes took Seconal with a whiskey chaser, a destructive practice. He continued to rewrite *Camino Real*, now a full-length play made up of journeying and surreal scenes. In spite of taking alcohol with prescription drugs, Williams finished his next major play, *Cat on a Hot Tin Roof*, in 1953.

DECEPTION AND GREED

Examining *Cat on a Hot Tin Roof*

During the 1950s, Tennessee Williams wrote about two difficult subjects that were seldom mentioned on the American stage: homosexuality and cancer. Being open about one's sexual orientation at this time was difficult. Williams never hid his gay life. However, he doubted that the public was ready to explore the subject in his plays. Incurable illness and a crude, overbearing father figure were also subjects that might put off an audience.

A play about a prep-school boy struggling with being gay opened on Broadway in 1953. *Tea and Sympathy* by Robert Anderson received a good reception. Williams, encouraged, finished *Cat on a Hot Tin Roof* and gave it to his agent.

Williams did obscure the nature of the love that the hero Brick felt for his dead friend Skipper. In an interview for *Theatre Arts* magazine in July 1955, Williams stated:

"Brick is definitely not a homosexual . . . Brick's self pity and recourse to the bottle are not the result of a guilty conscience in that regard."[1] Williams said that Brick's bitterness about the tragedy of Skipper's death was what made him drink, "although I do suggest that at least at some time in his life, there have been unrealized abnormal tendencies."[2]

Cat on a Hot Tin Roof opened in New York in March 1955. It won both the New York Drama Critics Circle Award and the Pulitzer prize. Yet Williams was not satisfied. Twenty years later, the times were right for a revision of this play. It is this final version that further defines the characters. The 1974–1975 Broadway revival script is the one most commonly produced today.

A BIRTHDAY PARTY GONE BAD

The plot of *Cat* spans the time of a birthday party on the expansive Pollitt plantation in the Mississippi Delta. Big Daddy Pollitt is turning sixty-five. His wife, Ida (called Big Mama), his elder son, Gooper, and his wife, Mae, plus their five small children and assorted friends and servants, throw him a celebration. The action never leaves the bedroom of Brick Pollitt, the younger son, and his wife, Margaret, called Maggie. Signs of the celebration are seen off an open gallery and heard from offstage.

The action will be driven by the goals of the three main characters. Brick's goal is to drown his present pain in alcohol. Maggie's goal is to win back her husband's love and sexual attention, as well as to secure his inheritance. Big Daddy's goal is to beat cancer, then spend the rest of his life as tyrannical master of his vast holdings.

The three secondary characters have their goals as well. Brother Gooper, a Memphis lawyer, and Mae, his grasping wife, are determined the Pollitt plantation should be theirs to run after Big Daddy dies. Ida Pollitt's main goal is to keep her husband alive, even though on most levels he rejects her. She also wants to keep the plantation in her own hands.

These six characters clash over and over throughout the course of the birthday party. At Blanche's birthday party in *Streetcar Named Desire*, the one invited guest fails to show up. This time, far too many guests arrive to win the favor of Big Daddy Pollitt.

The major characters must search for painful truths about who they really are. Longtime communication barriers between Brick and his wife, and Brick and his father, must be broken down. Williams describes their coming together as "a thundercloud of a common crisis."[3] As summer lightning and rumbling thunder threaten outside the house, explosive storms take place within.

THE IMPACT OF GHOSTS

The play deals with three ghosts, spirits of dead friends that impact Brick, Maggie, and Big Daddy. Skipper was Brick's best friend and football teammate. His love for

Brick and his death after Brick's desertion make him a character that still influences this story. Skipper not only haunts Brick, but also Maggie, who slept with him so he might "prove" he did not desire Brick physically. Her guilty act helped destroy him.

Two other ghosts, Jack Straw and Peter Uchello, were the farmers who gave Big Daddy his start on the plantation. They were also a homosexual couple that shared a bed in the same room now used by Brick and Maggie. Big Daddy understood these men. He tells Brick: "When Jack Straw died, why old Peter Uchello quit eatin' like a dog does when its master's dead, and died too."[4] Is it possible the ghosts of Straw and Uchello reflect the relationship of Brick and Skipper? Williams says Brick explodes as if "a quiet mountain blew suddenly up in volcanic flame," and accuses his father of asking if he and Skipper "did— sodomy—together?"[5] Brick's strong denial is accepted by Big Daddy.

During the last act, Big Daddy faces his favored son's misery over his lost glory and guilt about loving but failing Skipper. Brick then tells his father that they have hidden the truth from him. Big Daddy has inoperable cancer, and he will die soon. Brick must still grapple with his alcoholism, guilt, and crisis of self-identity. Maggie takes charge at the play's finale. She bitterly fights with Gooper and Mae, defending Brick's right to the estate. Her strength and female determination to draw Brick back and conceive his child make her the triumphant survivor in the end.

Williams once said that he heard the expression "nervous as a cat on a hot tin roof" from his father. This colorful picture was a good image for Margaret Pollitt. She reflects the powerful life force of the cat. So Williams used it to title this play.

STRONG ORIGINAL CHARACTERS

Maggie is a beautiful young woman with a powerful need for love and financial and social security. Although Southern women of the mid-twentieth century were expected to be gentle and retiring, Maggie cannot behave that way. Maggie admits that she has been forced to undergo "this hideous transformation, become—hard! Frantic!—cruel! . . . I can't afford to be thin-skinned any-more."[6] Maggie will not let Brick throw away his inheritance. She was "born poor, raised poor," and believes it is impossible to grow old with no money. She bluntly tells Brick that there are family members who want to cut them out because "you drink and I've borne no children."[7] Critic Dianne Cafagna says of her: "Maggie, like cancer, is the harsh reality the Pollitt family must learn to live with."[8]

Maggie has been trying to seduce her own husband because Brick clings to his drinking instead of his wife. Her beauty attracts other men, she tells Brick. Yet she wants no one but him. Claiming he is unnaturally

71

Big Daddy confronts Brick in the Hartford Stage Company's 2005 production of *Cat on a Hot Tin Roof*.

attached to his late friend, she cries: "Skipper is dead! I'm alive. Maggie the cat is alive!"[9]

Throughout the play, Brick reveals his prehistory. He was a handsome, talented football quarterback at the University of Mississippi. There he fell in love with Maggie and grew deeply involved with teammate Skipper. Not able to give up their glory days on the field, Brick and Skipper joined with others to form a semiprofessional team. Brick recalls keeping up "the aerial attack that made us famous."[10]

After Brick suffers an injury and can no longer play, Skipper falls apart without him. Brick tries sports announcing, but his depression and alcoholism keep him from being a success. He retreats to his parents' home, where he is forced to fend off his wife, his brother, and his father. Saying he "hates mendacity," or untruthfulness, Brick finally must spit out the truth of his refusing Skipper's love for him. His lack of courage and self-knowledge made Skipper slide into alcoholism and suicide.

Big Daddy Pollitt is an unusual character in American literature. He is a self-made man, who had to quit school at ten and work doggedly until he became overseer for Straw and Uchello. Usually such self-made men are admirable. Big Daddy is coarse, proud, vulgar, blunt, and self-centered. We meet him when he has been facing cancer, which in the 1950s was almost always fatal. A false report is given him on his birthday that claims he has no more than a spastic colon. However, everyone but him and his wife knows the truth. A fresh lease on life causes him to reach out to Brick, the one person in his life he actually cares for. During this process, he cruelly rejects his wife and older son.

Big Daddy does possess honesty and emotional courage. He is willing to go the distance with Brick to get to the bottom of his drinking and despair. Once Brick blurts out the truth of his malignant cancer, Big Daddy finds the strength to face his own death.

THE MEANINGS OF LOVE ARE EXPLORED

In the stage directions for *Cat*, Tennessee Williams said he intended to "catch the true quality of experience in a group of people." These people happen to be in the same family. Each of them lead what Williams termed tortured inner lives. Both Maggie and Big Mama are women who can love openly and endure the slights they get from their men. The love experienced by the three married couples is revealed to be quite different. A father's varying love for sons who are distant and even threatening to him is explored. The deep and forbidden love Skipper felt for Brick is brought out into the open. The difference between sexual attraction, need, and pure affection is painfully portrayed.

A FAMILY FILLED WITH MENDACITY

There are no inner monologues in *Cat*, as in previous Williams's plays. These characters verbally blast each other out loud. They demand truth. Big Daddy does not care if his truth telling hurts people. However, others lie for various reasons. Gooper and Mae lie to Big Daddy about his cancer so they can get through his birthday and court his favor. Maggie lies to Big Daddy about being pregnant, because she badly wants the lie to become truth. Saddest of all is Brick's lying to himself. He was unable to accept the unquestioning love he got from Skipper. Now he admits that he knew Skipper loved him—but he denied Skipper to the end.

Both Big Daddy and Brick, when told by their wives at separate times that they really love them, say "wouldn't it be funny if it were true?" Williams shows us men who have never been able to fully love and who are unable to accept unconditional love in return. The Pollitt family, like the Wingfield family in *The Glass Menagerie*, are universal. Although they love one another, they also deceive, deny, and hide feelings from one another. In the end, they do the best they can to go on.

MONEY CANNOT BUY YOU LOVE

A final theme in *Cat* is an exploration of the role of money and power. Williams knew wealthy plantation owners in Mississippi. He wrote *Cat* after he himself earned his way out of poverty and was financially secure. He realized that like Big Daddy Pollitt, people often used their money and power to buy attention and affection. He also knew, as

Maggie Pollitt says, that it is not so terrible to be poor when you are young and beautiful. Yet when you get older, Williams indicates it becomes impossible to bear.

CRITICS HOWL FOR CAT

Walter Kerr, writing for the *New York Herald Tribune*, called *Cat on a Hot Tin Roof* "a beautifully written, perfectly directed, stunningly acted play of evasions."[11] He wrote that in spite of every major character's search for truth, the play ends by evading it. Brooks Atkinson, writing for *The New York Times*, said one of the play's "great achievements is the honesty and simplicity of the craftsmanship. It seems not to have been written. It is . . . the basic truth . . . it is not only part of the truth of life: it is the absolute truth of the theatre."[12] Yet Atkinson recognizes the evasions of the play. He said of the main characters: "[L]ies are the only refuge they have from the ugly truths that possess their minds."[13]

Not every critic admired the play's veracity or appreciated the frankness of the characters. Robert Coleman from the New York *Daily Mirror* said that "much of the language is right from the barnyard . . . but these people are anything but aristocrats and much less than decent. They are neurotic, frustrated, and fascinated by bawdy speech."[14] Coleman feels the characters are "disturbed and disturbing people, tired of living and scared of dying."[15] The actors were praised for generating real emotion and excitement and the author recognized for creating almost operatic monologues and dialogues.

When the play had revivals on Broadway in 1975, in London in 2001, and in New York in 2003–2004, critics assessed the revised script and liked it. As London critic Lizzie Loveridge said in 2001, "The near half century has seen attitude changes towards gender but this play still works. Families still battle over inheritance. Sexually dysfunctional marriages still exist. Men and women still abuse each other. This production . . . deserves to be a highlight of the London theatrical year."[16]

BODY AND SOUL

Examining *Summer and Smoke*, *The Rose Tattoo*, and *The Night of the Iguana*

Not every play produced by Tennessee Williams was a smash hit on Broadway. *Summer and Smoke* opened on Broadway in October 6, 1948, and ran only three months. Some critics called it pretentious, boring, too long, and too dependent on the emotions. Only Brooks Atkinson of *The New York Times* saw its beauty, poetry, and artistry, and blamed Margo Jones's direction for its faults.

Williams was not satisfied with this work. He completely revised and published it in 1964 as *The Eccentricities of a Nightingale*. This version was done successfully on Broadway in 1971. Both plays are set in Glorious Hill, Mississippi, between 1900 and 1916.

The Rose Tattoo was produced on Broadway in 1951. It portrays life in a community of Sicilian Americans on the Gulf Coast near New Orleans. *The Night of the Iguana* opened on Broadway in 1961. It takes place in the steamy summer of 1940, located in the fictional Mexican resort town of Puerto Barrio.

These three plays are considered the most important of Williams's work after *The Glass Menagerie*, *A Streetcar Named Desire*, and *Cat on a Hot Tin Roof*. Although these plays were not as wildly successful financially as the first three, they show a broad artistic vision and have remained popular. Each became an honored film.

The Glass Menagerie and *A Streetcar Named Desire* were signed to lucrative Hollywood contracts. Theater companies around the world were producing them. Tennessee Williams became a rich playwright by age thirty-nine. His lifestyle had become one of restless roaming, from writing retreats in the South to rehearsal halls in the North. His holidays were usually spent in southern Europe. The only real estate Williams owned was his simple home on Duncan Street, Key West, Florida.

In 1950, Williams published his only novel, *The Roman Spring of Mrs. Stone*, about the emotional breakdown of an American widow who falls for a Roman gigolo. Mrs. Stone in many ways reflects the troubles visited on Williams himself. The stress of life as a celebrity playwright took a toll on him.

COMMON THEMES IN *SMOKE*, *TATTOO*, AND *IGUANA*

In the 1940s and 1950s, Williams was interested in writing about the *Good Woman versus the Fallen Woman*.

American morality demanded that to be a good woman, one must be pure before marriage and faithful to one's spouse after marriage. A woman who gives in to lust and passion outside of marriage is considered a fallen woman.

Alma Winemiller, the repressed minister's daughter in *Summer and Smoke*, is a good woman. Serefina della Rosa of *The Rose Tattoo*, the child bride who for her fifteen-year marriage gave herself solely to her husband, is a good woman. Hannah Jelkes, the unwed painter who devoted her life to art and to caring for her grandfather in *The Night of the Iguana*, is a good woman. In these characters, we see a woman who holds her needs and passions in check. However, each of these strong female characters is special. They live in different times and cultures and have unique personalities.

Each of these three plays also features a fallen woman who embraces sex outside of marriage. In *Summer and Smoke*, we meet Rosa Gonzales, who gives herself to John Buchanan in the hopes of improving her lot in life. We also meet Estelle in *The Rose Tattoo*, and later hear her voice admit she had an affair with Serefina's husband. Maxine in *The Night of the Iguana* is a major character, lusty and newly widowed. Maxine contents herself with casual sex with the boys who work for her. If Reverend Lawrence Shannon will be her lover, she will take in the fallen cleric.

The second common theme is the *role of religion* in a relationship. Alma, Serefina, and even Hannah are believers in God. Alma is a fine singer and a role model in her father's Protestant church. Serefina is childlike in her faith but a follower of the Catholic Church and its Holy Virgin Mary. Hannah searches for God in art, nature, people, even her grandfather's poem. However, the men that these women desire stray from their moral code. They are fighting a battle between body and soul. Each play studies how the need for these men affects these women in their beliefs.

Finally, Williams considers the *decline of innocence* as people head toward the end of their life. Purity gives way to corruption. Williams wrote in one of his last plays (*Something Cloudy, Something Clear*, 1981) a verse on this subject. His character August says: "God give me death before thirty, before my clean heart has grown dirty, soiled with the dust of much living, more wanting and taking than giving."[1] Alma knows that Doctor John has lost his moral direction through meaningless sexual affairs. Serefina discovers her adored husband, Rosario, cheated on her. Hannah's friend Reverend Shannon is near suicide due to the demise of his personal honor and faith. How these women react to this makes for great drama.

SMOKE OF A BURNING HEART

Williams lays out the stage carefully for *Summer and Smoke*. In the center is the town fountain. It is the statue of an angel with the inscription "Eternity." On one side is the Episcopal rectory. On the other side is Doctor Buchanan's home and medical office. Alma's father,

81

Reverend Winemiller, treats the spirit. John Buchanan and his father treat the body. The angel in between pours forth pure healing water and hope.

Although we meet Alma and John briefly when they are adolescents in the Prologue, the play presents them in their twenties. Alma speaks and acts as if she were much older. She had to replace her mother as the "wife" of the Rectory because her mother is emotionally disturbed. Alma has always been attracted to John. Yet she tends to put men off by being too nervous, judgmental, and repressed.

John is drawn to Alma but cannot relate to her. His need for physical satisfaction is met by Rosa Gonzalez, the daughter of the owner of the Moon Lake Casino. Critic Thomas P. Adler says that Alma and John constantly misread each other. "Neither one knows until very late in the play what it means to be a fully integrated human being."[2]

Balance between natural sexual attraction and good moral conduct is difficult for Alma and John to achieve. They have many gifts but seem to squander them in their search for self-identity. Alma tells John that love is not just coupling: "[T]here are some women, John, who can bring their hearts to it, also—who can bring their souls to it!"[3] John replies by giving Alma an anatomy lesson. He explains the brain is hungry for truth, the belly needs nourishment, and the sex part is hungry for love. "You've fed none—nothing. Love or truth . . . nothing but hand-me-down notions."[4]

Later, Alma confesses to Doctor John that she has been so disoriented and repressed that she thought she was dying. "But now the Gulf wind has blown that feeling away, like a cloud of smoke."[5] She yearns to love John with body and spirit. For John, their love is too late. He has put his image of Alma back up on the pedestal, like the angel's statue, and given his pledge to the younger, passionate but innocent Nellie.

Alma must swallow her rejection and frustration with her newly recognized sexuality. At the play's end, Alma is determined to try having relationships with men. She accepts a date with a man for the Moon Lake Casino, saluting the angel as she leaves.

The New York Times critic Brooks Atkinson said about the playwright in his review: "The twin themes of his tone poem are clearly stated: spirit and flesh, order and anarchy. He has caught them in the troubled brooding of two human hearts."[6] After its modest run on Broadway, *Summer and Smoke* was revived. On April 24, 1952, it opened at the Circle in the Square, a repertory company in Greenwich Village. This version starring young Geraldine Page was a solid hit. Because it was a major work playing in a theater downtown, people began calling it Off-Broadway theater.

Williams later reflected about all his heroines: "I think the character I like most is Miss Alma. She is my favorite because I came out so late [sexually] and so did Alma . . . Miss Alma grew up in the shadow of the rectory, and so did I."[7]

LOVE AND COMEDY COMBINE IN *ROSE TATTOO*

Williams chose a potentially serious subject, the devastating loss of a beloved husband and the problem of raising a teenage daughter alone. However, his treatment is warm, folksy, and often comic. The success of *The Rose Tattoo* depends on the audience believing in the widowed seamstress Serefina. She has clung to her grieving widow's role for three years. Serefina's Sicilian friends and her suitor, the warmly humorous truck driver Alvaro, must also be believable. Often the characters seem childlike, impulsive, and foreign to a mid-twentieth-century audience. Williams admitted the people in *Rose Tattoo* were acting on instinct, not always on reason. As critic Brooks Atkinson commented, "[T]hose gusty and volatile Sicilians blow hot and cold at bewildering speed."[8] Atkinson also recognized that Serefina makes the entire play work, as she "speaks the autobiography of her soul."[9]

Parallel characters to Serefina and Alvaro are Serefina's teenage daughter, Rosa, and her young sailor, Jack Hunter. Rosa, bright and pretty, is about to graduate from high school. She explodes with passionate love for Jack. Serefina will not let her daughter go out with a man unless they are engaged! Jack vows that not only will he respect Rosa's virginity, but that he is a virgin too. Finally, they are freed from Serefina's fearful grasp.

The voices of the Sicilian community include Father DeLeo the priest, Strega the neighborhood sorceress, and

84

Tennessee Williams reads his latest play to his grandfather, Reverend Walter Dakin, during one of his visits to New York. Dakin served as the inspiration for Hannah's grandfather, Nonno, in *Night of the Iguana*.

a trio of gossipy neighbor women and their raucous children. They keep Serefina grounded as she endures the hard truth of her husband's adultery, his murder due to drug smuggling, and the near loss of her faith. Serefina's rebirth as a woman only thirty years old is the triumphant ending to this warm human comedy. By accepting Alvaro's affection, Serefina becomes vital and able to love again.

THE NIGHT OF THE IGUANA SHOWS PEOPLE ON THE EDGE

This complex drama was Williams's last great Broadway triumph. Although *Summer and Smoke* and *Rose Tattoo* present American villages for the cast to inhabit, *The Night of the Iguana* creates a strange world all its own. In 1940, Maxine is managing the Costa Verde Hotel with her Mexican boy assistants. Into the hilltop resort come groups from other worlds: Nazis from Germany, Baptist teachers from Texas led by the desperately troubled Reverend Shannon, and Hannah and her ninety-seven-year-old grandfather, Nonno, from Nantucket and everywhere. Williams asks his audience to quickly accept this crowd. The survivors must be separated from those who are at the end of their tether.

When we get to know Shannon and Hannah, we realize they once had other options. Yet they were compelled to roam and search, until they ran out of money and survival tactics. Williams called Shannon, Hannah, and Nonno world-conquered protagonists. Shannon fights the "spooks" of depression and alcoholism, while Hannah quietly sips opium tea. Shannon quit being a true minister because of "fornication and heresy, in the same week."[10] His doubt and distrust of God and his weakness for girls have driven him to a breakdown. Hannah asks to lead him beside still waters. She has little else to give him. Yet Shannon calls her a real lady, and a great one.

As the play nears a climax, Shannon is tied to the crossbar of a hammock, for he threatens suicide. Hannah accuses him of putting on a "Passion Play" performance. He is atoning for his sins here instead of on a cross with nails. However, her kindness, strength, and understanding give Shannon hope. She echoes the author's personal moral code by saying: "Nothing human disgusts me, unless it's unkind, violent."

Nonno finally completes his last great poem, a plea for courage in the face of the natural corruption and decay of mankind. Shannon agrees to Hannah's request: [H]e cuts loose the iguana tied up to be eaten by the boys, "so that one of God's creatures could scramble home safe and free . . . a little act of grace."[11] At the play's end, Shannon compromises himself for a safe life with Maxine. Nonno has passed away. Hannah looks to God for rest and peace at last.

Critic Howard Taubman saw Williams "writing at the top of his form" in this play. "He is still grappling with the human mysteries that have always haunted him."[12] Taubman concludes that the play is eloquent in "declaring its respect for those who have to fight for their bit of decency."

SYMBOLS RIGHT UP TOP

Each of these three plays is rich in symbolism and metaphor. The primary symbols cannot be missed, because Tennessee Williams puts them in the titles.

Summer and Smoke refers to the long hot summer in Alma's life during which she kept herself chaste despite her love for John. Smoke results from a low, smoldering fire. Alma tells John: "[T]he girl who said 'no' doesn't exist any more, she died last summer—suffocated in smoke from something on fire inside her."[13] The slow burn of Alma's growing sexuality is also symbolized by the smoke.

The Rose Tattoo is referred to so often in this play that it almost becomes comic. Serefina's handsome husband had a rose tattooed on his chest, which so fascinated her that for a moment she saw it burn on her own. The rose was to Serefina the symbol of desire and conception of new life. By later in the play, when her prospective lover Alvaro tries to attract her, he gets a rose tattooed on his own chest. Serefina now feels *The Rose Tattoo* is just a ruse, a way to deceive her. In fact, her first husband was the deceiver, for he committed adultery. It is Alvaro that sincerely wants to be true to her. So what does the rose symbolize?

In this context, the rose can represent sexuality—purity—as well as the conception of a new life.

The Night of the Iguana refers both to the dark night of the spirit and to the captive lizard itself. In one sense, catching, fattening, and eating the iguana is a way of survival for the poor in Mexico. In another, the struggling iguana, says Shannon, is "at the end of its rope. Trying to go on past the end . . . like you! Like me! Like Grampa with his last poem!"[14] To free the iguana was a strike for freedom and hope for the future for Hannah and Shannon.

Religious and Christian spiritual symbols are found in all three plays. Alma sings hymns and drinks the Angel's water of eternal life. Yet she confronts her humanity, when John shows her the anatomy chart of the naked human body. Serefina lights candles to the Madonna, but refuses to see the light of truth about her husband. Shannon nearly strangles himself trying to yank off his gold cross. The bitter opium tea Hannah gives him is referred to as Christ's communion cup.

All of Williams's major plays studied so far have explored a wider range and depth of human character than the plays written by his contemporary playwrights. Williams said in an essay: "[T]he theater has made in our time its greatest artistic advance through the unlocking and lighting up and ventilation of the closets, attics, and basements of human behavior and experience."[15] Looking back, Williams was perhaps more important than any other author in creating this "lighting up" on stage.

89

CHAPTER 7

SHORT PLAYS AND OTHER WORKS

Other notable works by Tennessee Williams

When artists decide to do a large work, they often make a small sketch or model of a section of it. When composers begin a long piece, they may work on a short part or motif from it. Tennessee Williams worked in a similar way. When he wrote short stories or one-act plays, he did not necessarily mean them to be sketches or short parts of a major play. Yet he seemed to take characters, themes, actions, and motifs from his short works and use them as inspiration for his long ones.

WHY WILLIAMS WROTE ONE-ACT PLAYS

The Trinity Repertory Company is a professional theater in Providence, Rhode Island. In October 2005, Trinity Rep produced a revival of *Suddenly Last Summer*. Williams wrote this difficult, many-layered play in 1957 and 1958. It ran successfully on Broadway, paired with another short piece. The Trinity Rep cast of *Suddenly Last Summer* produced, as a gift to their theater fans, a performance of readings of Williams's one-act plays on October 29, 2005.

Director Laura Kepley spoke at this performance about why Williams's short plays are good to see. "In these short plays, you see prototypes of great characters he created," she said. They also provide a window into "the world of imagination he constructs."[1]

FIVE PLAYS MAKE A SHOW

The following plays were chosen by Kepley and the Trinity Rep cast. All but one of them were published by 1945, the year Williams had his first hit with *The Glass Menagerie*. While they prepare us for his future greatness, they also show Williams's present genius in bright short flashes.

The Lady of Larkspur Lotion (1945)

In darkly comic tone, Williams writes about his poor days in New Orleans's French Quarter. He introduces two renters of small ugly rooms on the edge of society. The Landlady (Mrs. Wire) is hard on both the Lady (Mrs. Hardwicke-Moore) and her neighbor the Writer, who owe her rent. The Lady maintains high-tone airs, dreams, and fantasies about support coming in from a Brazilian rubber plantation. The Landlady knows that the little money the

Lady gets is from men she entertains in her room. The Larkspur Lotion that the lady clings to is really cheap alcohol. Mrs. Wire calls both of them "Quarter rats, half-breeds, drunks, degenerates, who try to get by on promises, lies, delusions!"[2]

The Writer defends the Lady, and shouts at the landlady: "Suppose I wanted to be a great artist but lacked the force and the power? Suppose the curtains of my exalted fancy rose on magnificent dramas—but the house-lights darkened before the curtain fell!"[3] After ejecting the Landlady, the Writer confesses he likes to be called Mr. Chekhov. His compassion allows the Lady to dream on for another day.

The Lady is a precursor of Blanche DuBois in her attitudes, faded Southern gentility, and hidden sexuality. The Writer expresses Williams's own belief that artists need their dreams to escape from the hard cold lies of the real world. This theme will be expanded in several larger plays.

Talk to Me Like the Rain (1953)

This short work also looks at escape from the world's realities through art and dreams. The Man and the Woman are holed up in a rented room in New York, listening to the rain. The Man is probably a prostitute, a lost confused soul. He says he gets "passed around like a dirty postcard."[4] His long monologues are frightening and chaotic. For the Man, movies and books can be more real than his own grim experiences.

The Woman seems incapable of supporting herself and depends on the Man. Her vision of her life is a retreat into a hotel room where she is waited on with no one asking for any commitment. There she will read the days away. "It will be sweet and cool this friendship of mine with dead poets, for I won't have to touch them or answer their questions. They will talk to me and not expect me to answer."[5] The Woman's poetic image is the white clean wind that blows from the edge of the world. The end of her vision is to see her body disintegrate and have this wind whisk her away to a pure life after death.

Two people, battered by life, cannot find positive solutions. No dark humor gets them through the day. Yet they are there for each other. The characters use interior monologues and lyric diction. These devices will be developed and used effectively in Williams's major plays.

Hello from Bertha (1945)

This play provides an outstanding yet demanding role for a middle-aged actress. Bertha, an aging prostitute from the river flats of East St. Louis, is too exhausted mentally and emotionally to decide what to do with herself. The brothel's madam, called Goldie, wants Bertha to work or get out of the room. She needs it for other business. The tension that grows between Goldie and Bertha is gripping, yet darkly amusing.

Soon Bertha's fantasies are more real to her than her sordid life. She suffers from severe alcoholism and paranoia. Goldie knows Bertha needs hospitalization. Claiming Goldie will lock her up in "the city bug house," Bertha's moods flash from sentimental love for Charlie, the man she once worked for as a girl, to fury over a supposed robbery. Williams in his stage direction describes Bertha's condition as "schizophrenic suspicion."[6]

Another prostitute, Lena, comes in to check on Bertha, as she moves in and out of lucidity. Bertha dictates to Lena a letter, which simply says: "Hello from Bertha to Charlie— with all her love."[7]

Given the unlikelihood that Williams ever spent time in an East St. Louis brothel, the stark realism of Bertha's situation is truly believable. Sadly, Williams's sister, Rose, was being treated for severe mental illness during 1941, when this piece was written. Several major Williams's characters have echoed Bertha in their delusions and desperation.

This Property Is Condemned (1945)

A thirteen-year-old scarecrow of a girl named Willie is found wandering the railroad tracks. A fourteen-year-old boy called Tom, who has cut school to fly his kite, encounters her. The girl's unfolding story is bizarre. She longs for her dead older sister, Alva, whom she adored. Alva encouraged the child's fantasies. Wearing her sister's old velvet dress, Willie claims she will take over Alva's male admirers, the railroad men who slept with her. The child's odd perceptions, lack of values, and abandonment by her family become frightening. Yet Willie's perky personality gives us hope for her.

Like *The Lady of Larkspur Lotion*, *This Property* has off-beat humor. Willie is barely surviving on handouts and garbage, living in a condemned house. Yet her spirit and spunk is such that you feel hopeful for her. Williams captures the voice of an adolescent Delta country girl, a voice he never used again. The sense of abandonment, however, is explored by characters in later plays. The screenplay of this piece was produced in 1966. Young Francis Ford Coppola wrote the script, with an expanded story including everyone mentioned in the short play.

Williams uses repeated poetic images in *This Property Is Condemned*, which he will do again in larger works. Willie and Tom repeat the image of the sky as being "perfectly white. It's white as a clean piece of paper."[8] Willie also recalls her fifth-grade teacher giving her a "white piece of paper," to make a drawing. But Willie draws her own dark reality, her father being hit with a whiskey bottle. Willie recalls the image of white when she tells Tom her dying sister dreamed of getting "loads and loads of white flowers," like Greta Garbo got as *Camille*. Now Alva is in "the bone-orchard." The whiteness of bones completes the imagery, for whiteness is the symbol of hope, purity, and death.

The Unsatisfactory Supper (1945)
(Also titled The Long Stay Cut Short)

Along with the pathos of Aunt Rose, the aged servant, there is real humor between the married couple Baby Doll and Archie Lee in this Delta drama. They have passed Aunt Rose around the family like a piece of property. Now no one wants her because she cannot even boil greens properly.

Aunt Rose can be arch, dry, and humorous. The banter

95

PATHOS—*An element in creative art or experience that evokes sympathy, pity, and/or compassion.*

between Aunt Rose and her employers is darkly comic. At the end, Rose moves into senility, panic, and symbolically dies, blowing away in the wind. Rose echoes two of Williams's family members. Both his elderly grandmother and his sister, Rose, the most beloved people in Tom Williams's world, were unwelcome annoyances in Cornelius Williams's home.

Sometimes Tennessee Williams took a character and an incident in a short play, and incorporated them into a different larger work. For instance, his short play *27 Wagons Full of Cotton* features Silva Vicarro, the superintendent of the Syndicate Plantation in Blue Mountain, Mississippi. Vicarro has a large load of cotton to process. His cotton gin was mysteriously burned. So he must pay to use the one owned by Jake, the man we know was responsible for the arson. Jake's wife, Flora, keeps Vicarro "entertained" all day while Jake does the job. In his full-length screenplay, *Baby Doll* (1956), Williams used the Silva Vicarro character and the burning of the gin, but created a different direction to the story. He also radically changed Flora and created a servant similar to Aunt Rose.

During the past twenty years, there have been many productions of Tennessee Williams's short plays, grouped together to form an evening's entertainment. A New York production named *Ten by Tennessee* was termed "an opportunity to see an artist experiment and expand."[9]

Another production called *8 by Tenn* was done in 2003

by the Hartford Stage, Hartford, Connecticut. The program covered two evenings. Critic Karen Bovard wrote of these short works: "While many of them would be unsatisfying in isolation, together they offer a rare glimpse into the experimental variety Williams favored and for which he rarely receives credit."[10]

One of Williams's one-acts he wrote in 1948 was expanded into a long play that is unlike any others. He called it *Camino Real*. When it opened on Broadway in March 1953, a lot of Williams's political criticism was cut out. He had written of the unchecked power of capitalism and the activities of a government committee that investigated people's political and personal lives. The rest of the play, expressionistic and dreamlike in structure, was filled with literary figures like Casanova, Marguerite Gautier, or "Camille," Lord Byron, Kilroy, and Don Quixote. It also portrayed average people struggling through a hard life, such as gypsies, street cleaners, a loan shark, and vendors. In order to give the sense of freedom and flow, Williams said he had to pay "more conscious attention to form and construction than I have in any work before. Freedom is not achieved simply by working freely."[11]

After the Broadway audiences failed to flow along with Williams and this play as presented, he rewrote it his way. Several characters and scenes and presumably the more politically critical material were restored for its 1953 publication and remains today.

97

WILLIAMS IN THE STONED AGE

Tennessee Williams wrote a play called *The Milk Train Doesn't Stop Here* in 1963. It was written in conjunction with the dying of his devoted companion, Frank Merlo. Although this work failed on Broadway, the leading character of Flora Goforth may be closest to Williams's interior self. She expresses Williams's grief over Merlo's death and his guilt over their being estranged before Merlo was stricken with cancer.

In his *Memoirs*, Williams recalled: "What I didn't know was that I was as much in love with Frankie all that difficult time of the early Sixties as I had even been before."[12] After Merlo's death, Williams reflected: "[W]hen he ceased to be alive, I couldn't create a life for myself. So I went into a seven-year depression."[13] Williams referred to the sixties as "my stoned age."[14] His addiction to a combination of prescription drugs began to destroy him, a situation obvious to everyone close to him.

By 1969, Williams's brother, Dakin, tried two sincerely meant plans to help save his brother. Dakin encouraged Williams to be confirmed into the Roman Catholic Church, a religion he had joined when in the service. Then, Dakin forced Williams into Barnes Hospital in St. Louis for detoxification and therapy. The hospital staff felt he would be best treated in the psychiatric ward. This hospital stay was terrifying for Williams. He knew that both his sister and his mother had to be committed for mental

98

illness, and he feared his own mental breakdown. Dakin Williams's intervention may have saved his brother's life. Yet Williams said he was traumatized over it. He never accepted the good reasons why Dakin did this, and he broke relations with him.

After this treatment, Williams was able to go on writing. He wrote two full-length plays at this time: *Small Craft Warnings* (opened off Broadway April 2, 1972, then at the New Theatre in June 1972) and *Red Devil Battery Sign* (opened in Boston June 18, 1976). *Small Craft Warnings*, set in a seedy beachfront bar north of San Diego, is an expanded version of a one-act play called *Confessional*. Some of its characters are grounded, such as Monk the bar owner and Leona and Doc who are local residents. Others are drifting through. Doc tells Monk: "You are running a place of refuge for vulnerable human vessels."[15] Characters take turns in a "confessional area" under a special spotlight where they tell the audience directly how they feel about their lives. Three of the male characters are gay, and two take advantage sexually of unstable female characters. The language can be vulgar, the action violent. Tennessee Williams himself played the role of the drunken, unlicensed Doc in the first week's performances to excite business. The dark radical nature of the play failed to impress critics, but it intrigued audiences enough to give it a solid two-hundred-performance run.

Red Devil Battery Sign reflects some of the social and political concerns that Williams may have felt as far back as the 1950s. The theme is entrapment of people by their own needs and by the materialist industrial culture that runs America. Williams was actually forward-looking in the 1970s to envision how the mechanized world might soon paralyze human self-expression and interrelationships. Companies had begun to depend on computers. To a man who had always been suspicious of Big Business, this development was worrisome. A theme also runs through the play regarding America's deep military involvement in Vietnam, a situation Williams protested. Set in contemporary Dallas, the characters are given characteristic names like King. They are difficult to analyze and not always appealing. Yet the story is a fine attempt to define the role of secrets, money, and power in life. As Woman Downtown, the leading female character, says: "it talks, money talks, not heads, not hearts, not tongues of prophets or angels, but money does, oh money hollers, love."[16] *Red Devil Battery Sign* was produced in Boston, June 1976, and in London, June 1977. It has never had a Broadway production.

In the early seventies, Williams decided to write a deeply revealing autobiography. Working with editors from Doubleday and Company, he produced *Memoirs* in 1975. In this rambling, chaotic book, Williams gave shocking and blunt information about his emotional problems, addictions, and sexual habits. Critics wished it had revealed more about his writing life and career. It did capture much of Williams's dark humor and honesty.

The one constant thing in Williams's life was movement. He moved between his regular haunts of Key West,

New Orleans, and New York, running to Europe to see productions of his plays. Regularly he visited his sister, Rose, in her sanatorium in Ossining, New York. Sometimes he had Rose driven to New York City for a treat. In 1975, he told his longtime friends director Elia Kazan and actress Maureen Stapleton that his one obligation was to endure.

IN TWO LATE PLAYS, WILLIAMS GOES "HOME"

Two of Williams's home cities were the sites for late plays. *Vieux Carre* was set during Williams's beginning years in New Orleans. It ran well in London in 1978, but it was never a Broadway success. *A Lovely Sunday for Creve Coeur*, which opened off Broadway in 1979, was set in his old neighborhood in St. Louis. By setting *Creve Coeur* in the 1930s, Williams could use his personal memories of the city's social attitudes and locales.

A Lovely Sunday for Creve Coeur can be seen as a string quartet, made up of four women's voices. Dorothea, a lonely thirtyish high-school-civics teacher, speaks with the violin's melody. Bodey, nearly forty, a hardworking factory clerk, underscores a hardy bass. Art teacher Helena, an affected, snobbish spinster, insinuates the viola's sound. And Sophie Gluck, an emotionally disturbed, grieving girl living in Dorothea and Bodey's building, moans and cries like the cello. These four women are intertwined in their needs and goals. Some goals seem to be selfish, some driven by fear. By the drama's end, those who deserve lasting love and caring will receive it.

As this work was previewing in New York, Tennessee Williams joined a group interview for *New York Theatre Review*. Director Craig Anderson liked *A Lovely Sunday for Creve Coeur* because "the women are the most beautiful characterizations. This play is simply lovely in the way that the three women vie for each other's favor."[17] Williams recognized that these women were ordinary, down-to-earth Midwesterners. He did not write long speeches with poetic or lyrical imagery. He said, "If I had put lyricism into the mouths of any of those characters, it would have been out of character, it wouldn't have rung true."[18] This shows Williams never lost his clear regard for each character as a singular individual.

Williams was at work on the revision process on *Creve Coeur*. Director Anderson called him a "rewrite specialist," and claimed he gave more than is needed to cut away, "down to the bare bone of what needs to stay."[19] While Williams stated that "loneliness is the main theme," he also saw valor as a recurring characteristic in the play. He talked about Dorothea, who finally realizes her lover, Ralph, has used her sexually and then dumped her. Williams has Dorothea tell Sophie Gluck, "Now, Sophie, we just have to go on. That's all life seems to offer or demand, just go on."[20]

Williams himself went on, even when the core of his life, his plays, seemed to be rejected by the critics. In 1981, he gave an interview to his friend journalist Dotson Rader. He was at work on what would be his final full play, *A House Not Meant to Stand*. He told Rader: "When I write, I don't aim to shock people . . . I don't think that anything that occurs in life should be omitted from art, though the artist should present it in a fashion that is artistic and not ugly. I set out to tell the truth. And sometimes the truth is shocking."[21]

When Rader asked Williams how he regarded death, he said, "I have a very strong will. There were occasions in the last years when I might have gone out. But my will forces me to go on because I've got unfinished work."[22]

Tennessee Williams died late on the night of February 24, 1983. Police found him in his New York hotel suite, with a medicine bottle cap lodged inside his throat. Conflicting reports were published on what happened. However, Williams's death was ruled to have been a choking accident.

OTHER PLAYWRIGHTS

Influences and contemporaries of Williams

Tennessee Williams started pursuing playwriting and the world of theater in his twenties. His parents did not have the inclination to take him to the professional theater, although he probably attended productions of musicals at the St. Louis Muni Opera, a large outdoor amphitheater. His grandfather, Reverend Dakin, enjoyed reading dramatic literature to him. Williams's first love, however, was not drama. He studied and wrote poetry and short fiction all through school. He also wrote articles for newspapers. Tennessee Williams then changed his direction. He became such a dedicated playwright that he worked daily, no matter what his mental or physical health.

EARLY INFLUENCES

From 1929 to 1932 at the University of Missouri, Williams studied the dramas of August Strindberg and Henrik Ibsen. In his *Memoirs*, Williams says that during the summer of 1935, he was recovering from physical and mental exhaustion at his grandparents' home in Memphis. That summer, a Memphis theater group produced his first short play. He called it "a farcical but rather touching little comedy about two sailors on a date."[1] It was at that time, he said, "I fell in love with the writing of Anton Chekhov."[2] Although he found British poet and prose writer D. H. Lawrence an inspiration, Williams later claimed the Russian author "takes precedence as an influence—that is, if there has been any particular influence beside my own solitary bent."[3] Williams especially loved Chekhov's *The Seagull*, which he called the greatest of modern plays.

Anton Chekhov (1860–1904) was famed for both his short stories and full-length plays. Besides *The Seagull*, his most widely produced plays are *The Cherry Orchard*, *The Three Sisters*, and *Uncle Vanya*. Chekhov's characters are all small-town, middle-class folk. They are striving to move socially upward, lead a better life, and achieve goals. Yet they are trapped in their mundane rural existence. Based in nineteenth–century-Russian society, these characters are limited by their social and economic class as much as by their lack of drive.

Theater scholar Oscar G. Brockett said of Chekhov's plays: "The subtext is often as important as text. . . . The plays intermingle the comic, serious, pathetic, and ironic so thoroughly that they do not fit into any dramatic type."[4] Williams felt the sense of frustration and family misunderstanding that pervades Chekhov's plays. He used it in shaping his own dramatic work.

EUROPEAN MODERNISTS' INFLUENCE ON WILLIAMS

August Strindberg was considered a shocking radical by the turn of the twentieth century. He wrote plays exploring human relationships in a frank but realistic way. Few authors since Shakespeare had written about parental anger, sexual violence, and male-female struggles for power the way Strindberg did.

Henrik Ibsen took a different approach. He wrote about intense conflict between men and women, in an era when women were dominated by the males in their lives. He stripped away the exterior layer of people's social behavior. Forbidden subjects such as adultery, female suicide, divorce and family abandonment, and sexually transmitted diseases all figured in Ibsen's work.

Theater historian Peter Arnott said of Ibsen's play *A Doll's House* (1879–80), "So convincing was Ibsen's portrayal of a marriage that the audiences were shocked. This play seemed to reach into their own homes and threaten the foundations of society."[5] Ibsen's work was banned in his own country for many years. Williams found these writers liberating.

EUGENE O'NEILL: PREDECESSOR TO WILLIAMS

Williams was familiar with American playwright Eugene O'Neill's work. O'Neill was born in 1888 to a New York theater family. His father, James O'Neill, was a leading actor, and his brother also became one. Young Eugene was determined to write a new style of play, different from the melodramas and romances in which his father starred. O'Neill took classic stories and portrayed them in radical, unusual ways. By studying new European authors, O'Neill used their nonrealistic methods to bring out the desires and fears of his characters. Like Strindberg, he explored dream sequences. He showed minds fragmenting and human guilt destroying people. Sometimes he used masks on his actors. So the actors would pronounce each word the way he wanted, O'Neill wrote the dialect for many of his characters. Often he used long interior monologues to express a character's feelings. He experimented constantly with shape, form, and style.

Some of O'Neill's important plays of the 1920s are not often produced today. Two of them, *Strange Interlude* (1928) and *Mourning Becomes Electra* (1931) are extremely long and dark. Other works use stories from New England. The O'Neill family owned a cottage in New London, Connecticut, the only real home young Eugene knew. He absorbed the ways of New England seafarers and farmers and colorful characters like those he met in the New London waterfront bars. These people found their way into his plays.

Desire Under the Elms (1924) is an American retelling of a Greek tale of an old father, his beautiful younger new wife, and his adult sons. When the wife develops a passion for her stepson, tragedy is bound to happen. *A Moon for the Misbegotten, The Iceman Cometh*, and *Long Day's Journey Into Night* were all completed by 1940, when O'Neill fell ill. *Long Day's Journey* was not produced until after his death in 1953. It is a heartfelt study of O'Neill's frustrated, tyrannical father, sad morphine-addicted mother, and alcoholic older brother. The younger brother with tuberculosis represents himself. This hurtful family is trapped together in their New London cottage. O'Neill won every playwriting major award, including one that was never given to any other American dramatist: the Nobel Prize for Literature.

Did O'Neill influence Williams? In a 1981 interview, Williams said: "I liked O'Neill's writing. He had . . . a great sense of drama, yes. But most of all, it was his spirit, his passion, that moved me."[6] O'Neill proved that America could produce a great, enduring, original playwright. He must have given Williams hope to go on.

WILLIAM INGE AND ARTHUR MILLER: WILLIAMS'S CONTEMPORARIES

Two years after Tennessee Williams was born in 1911 in Columbus, Mississippi, William Inge was born and raised in Independence, Kansas. In 1915, Arthur Miller was born in New York City and raised in Brooklyn. These three writers came from different regions, different backgrounds, and different religions. Yet they ended up producing Broadway shows and outstanding films that competed with and complemented each other for decades.

William Inge, like Williams and Miller, knew early in his life he wanted to be a writer. Inge earned college degrees in Lawrence, Kansas, and Nashville, Tennessee, and taught both high school and college drama courses. Inge crossed paths with Tennessee Williams when Williams was still Tom in St. Louis. As a St. Louis newspaper drama critic, Inge reviewed Williams's plays and admired him. He went to Chicago to review *The Glass Menagerie*. He later said, "I was so moved by the play . . . I thought it was the finest play I had seen in many years. I went home to St. Louis and felt, 'Well, I've got to write a play.'"[7]

Inge's play *Come Back, Little Sheba*, opened on Broadway in 1950. Inge, like Williams, wrote about interpersonal relationships in humble homes. His intimate knowledge and understanding of people he credited to his family and friends in Independence. He said: "Big people come out of small towns."[8] *Come Back, Little Sheba*, a drama that brought lead actress Shirley Booth the Tony Award, centers on a middle-aged couple who had an early marriage because the lady was pregnant. "Doc" Delaney, a reformed alcoholic, had to give up medical school and support Lola, who lost the baby at birth. After years of dreary marriage, in which Lola heaped her affection on her little dog, Sheba, the couple rents a room to a beautiful college girl—and the inevitable sexual explosion occurs.

Williams admired Inge's work. He told Dotson Rader: "*Come Back, Little Sheba* was a brilliant play. That's why I introduced him to Audrey Wood."[9] Wood became Inge's agent, and promoted his career with the same drive she gave to Williams.

In 1953, Inge's play *Picnic* ran on Broadway, winning the Pulitzer prize, New York Drama Critics Circle Award, and many others. This warm family drama centered on women in a small Kansas town affected by the arrival of an attractive male stranger. Inge portrayed simple people who were deeply intertwined in one another's lives.

In 1955, Inge saw his play *Bus Stop* open on Broadway. A midwestern comedy/drama about a handful of drifting souls stuck in a roadside café during a snowstorm, *Bus Stop* touched critics and audiences. It is perhaps his most revived play. *The Dark at the Top of the Stairs*, a 1957 autobiographical work in which Inge tried to use family experiences, was a great critical success. Inge's 1959 play *A Loss of Roses* did not please the critics and had a short run. Inge's tendency toward alcoholism and depression began to affect him.

Inge, like Williams, tried films. His original screenplay, *Splendor in the Grass*, starred young Natalie Wood, and in his first screen role, Warren Beatty. Inge himself played the small role of Reverend Whitman. Dealing with some of Tennessee Williams's favorite subjects—the battle in a young respectable girl to control her sexual passion, and the huge pressure placed on the favored son to carry on his father's dreams—Inge's characters were movingly portrayed. In 1960, the film's star Natalie Wood was nominated for Best Actress. Although she lost, Inge won the Academy Award for Best Original Screenplay.

Continuing as a playwright, Inge moved to California to teach. After writing two autobiographical novels, Inge succumbed to depression and alcoholism. He committed suicide in 1973.

Arthur Miller had a strong, varied career that lasted throughout the twentieth century until his death in 2005. After graduating from University of Michigan with some playwriting awards in hand, Miller returned to his native New York City. He married in 1940 and worked on building ships in the Brooklyn Navy Yard during World War II. The WPA's Federal Theatre Project gave him work as a radio scriptwriter. Although his first play done in New York was not successful, it won the Theatre Guild National Prize.

During 1945, Miller published his first novel, *Focus*. At this time, he saw *A Glass Menagerie* on Broadway. Miller said in a 1984 interview soon after Williams's death that this play "lifted lyricism to its highest level in our theatre's history . . . what was new in Tennessee Williams was his rhapsodic insistence that form serve his utterance rather than dominating and cramping it."[10] Williams showed that poor common people like the Wingfield family could be eloquent and moving.

Miller wrote *All My Sons* in 1947, his first hit on Broadway. Also heavily influenced by Ibsen's plays, Miller showed his characters' prehistory in the way Ibsen did.

Tennessee Williams (left) with director Elia Kazan (center) and fellow playwright Arthur Miller (right) at a book-signing event held at Brentano's bookstore in New York City in February 1967.

Since he was writing about the consequences of men's actions, he needed to show what they had done before they appeared in the play's present. The play also explored the theme of the impact of a lost son.

In 1949, Miller's next important play, *Death of a Salesman*, opened. The Salesman is Willy Loman, an older man who traveled New England to promote a company's products to dealers. Using a technique Miller might have seen in O'Neill's early plays, he has Willy Loman hear and speak to people from his past. Willy and the audience see these people, but no one else on stage does. This ranting leads his wife and sons to fear he is losing his mind. The decline and fall of Willy Loman, who determines all self-worth by being financially successful and being well liked, becomes an American tragedy. This play brought Miller the Drama Critics Circle award and the Pulitzer prize.

The Crucible opened on Broadway in 1952. Miller had studied historic accounts of the Salem, Massachusetts, witch trials. He created a dramatic account of a Salem witch hunt to parallel an investigation of supposed Communists being done in 1950 by the House Un-American Activities Committee in Washington. Critic Raymond Williams says about *The Crucible*: "Miller brilliantly expresses a particular crisis—the modern witch hunt—in his own society. . . . It is not often that issues and statements so clearly emerge in a naturally dramatic form."[11] *The Crucible* won the Tony and the Donaldson Prize for 1953, and is often revived today.

In 1947, Miller wrote a one-act play based on a

supposedly true story of an Italian longshoreman who informed on an illegal alien relative. In 1955, *A View from the Bridge*, paired with another one-act called *A Memory of Two Mondays*, opened on Broadway. Although it ran for 158 performances, critics did not care for what they called a cold and unengaging play. Miller expanded *A View from the Bridge* into a conventional two-act, and took it to London, where it was a hit with a new ending in which the informer protagonist Eddie is forgiven by his wife. Miller then took the play to Paris, where he wrote a third ending, in which Eddie commits suicide. Like Tennessee Williams, Miller was fascinated with ethnic culture (see *A Rose Tattoo*) and with revising his work.

Miller continued to write for decades. *After the Fall*, about his marriage to movie star Marilyn Monroe, and *Incident at Vichy* (1964), reflecting his views of anti-Jewish behavior, were both produced in New York. He wrote *The Price* in 1968, which was a Broadway success. *The Creation of the World and Other Business* (1972), and *The American Clock* (1980) also had New York runs. Although his original screenplay *The Misfits* was not a success, his script *Playing for Time*, produced as a television film in 1980, was acclaimed. It portrayed the determination of concentration-camp women to stay alive by playing in an orchestra for their vicious captors.

In 1994, Miller saw his psychological drama *Broken Glass* premiere. This play unravels the many reasons why a Jewish New Yorker in 1938 may find her legs paralyzed. Miller explores the effects on his protagonist Sylvia of

114

Nazi anti-Semitism, a husband who has turned his back on his Jewish identity, and a desperate need for attention. In 2000, Miller's final major work, *The Ride Down Mount Morgan*, appeared on Broadway. A tale of a rich and self-centered man who secretly juggles two wives and families, *The Ride* was both tragic and darkly comic at the same time.

A UNIQUE CONTEMPORARY: EDWARD ALBEE

Born in 1928, Edward Albee was living in New York City during the 1950s when Williams, Inge, and Miller were hit playwrights. Albee was the adopted only child of the wealthy Albee family of Larchmont, New York, owners of a chain of theaters. Young Edward had a troubled youth. He disliked his parents, performed badly at several private high schools, and dropped out of college after his freshman year. Unlike Williams, who spent his twenties trying to write while nearly starving, Albee had a small monthly inheritance on which to survive. Albee studied Williams's work and that of all twentieth-century playwrights. Then he found his own unique style and voice.

Albee could be called a *selective realist* in the way that O'Neill, Miller, and Williams are. Selective realism is seen when a playwright sets his play in a real place, such as a house, a garden, a park, the beach, etc. He uses real people as characters. He then uses certain details of dialogue, sets, lights, or action in a way that is *not* realistic. Having the character Tom move back and forth between Narrator and family character in *The Glass Menagerie*, or having someone speak to or hear from others that are not present like Willie Loman does in *Death of a Salesman*, creates selective realism. Albee took this style to another level. He added the *absurdist* element. This meant that certain realistic characters suddenly say or do abnormal, nonsensical things. Absurdist writers use as a theme the lack of logic or sense in much of human relationships.

Albee's first works were short plays. In some ways they were funny, touching, even frightening. *The Zoo Story* opened off Broadway in January 1960. In April 1960, *The Sandbox* opened off Broadway and *The Death of Bessie Smith* opened in Berlin. These plays were filled with sharp dialogue and black humor. Critic and biographer Mel Gussow called *The Zoo Story* "a report from the front line of urban life and death."[12]

Nothing from these short plays quite prepared the theater world for Albee's first major work, *Who's Afraid of Virginia Woolf?* This lengthy three-act play opened on Broadway in the fall of 1962. It is set on a college campus (although Albee only spent a year and a half at Trinity College in Hartford, Connecticut) and explores an intense, bizarre marriage (although Albee was homosexual).

A long-married academic couple employs cruel games during an evening of heavy drinking with a new, young professor and his wife. We see that the older couple

(George and Martha) cannot go on together without fights, humiliations, victories, and illusions. Albee said about this couple: "George and Martha enjoyed their verbal duels with each other, and while they were deadly serious, they were always . . . in admiration of each other's skills."[13]

The most baffling illusion George and Martha create is Sonny-Jim, their secret child, who represents the one pure thing between them. Suddenly Martha drags him out in front of young couple Nick and Honey. Once this "son" was the glue in their barren marriage. Now that he is exposed, he must be expelled. Will Martha and George survive as a couple? After their long evening of cruelty, Martha says to Nick: "George . . . who keeps learning the games we play as quickly as I can change the rules; who can make me happy and I do not wish to be happy, and yes I do wish to be happy. George and Martha . . . sad, sad, sad."[14] The play closes with Martha clinging to George. We cannot be certain of their future.

Albee has written many other plays on a variety of issues during his forty-year career. His themes have covered the breakdown in human communication (*Seascape*), man's attempt to understand God (*Tiny Alice*), and the many views of a woman's life (*Three Tall Women*). In a recent play, *Sylvia*, or *The Goat*, Albee creates a solid prosperous unit of the Husband, Wife, Son, and Best Friend. He then pushes them over the edge, when the Husband develops a deep passion outside his marriage. This common infidelity becomes absurd and frightening when we find out his passion is for a docile goat called Sylvia. Albee continues his work as both author and teacher at this writing.

Eugene O'Neill, William Inge, Arthur Miller, Edward Albee, and Tennessee Williams created a body of theatrical work that has represented twentieth-century America. This work lives in theaters in America and around the world.

WILLIAMS LIVES ON

The legacy of Tennessee Williams

Experiencing the dramatic works of Tennessee Williams can be done in three ways. One can attend a staged production. One can read the text and imagine how a staged production would look. Or, one can study a film version. Fifteen of Williams's works have been made into major films. One, *Baby Doll*, combined two early short plays, and after being written as a film script, morphed into a full-length stage play. Williams himself worked on screenplays for *The Glass Menagerie*, *A Streetcar Named Desire*, *The Rose Tattoo*, *Baby Doll*, *The Fugitive Kind*, *Suddenly Last Summer*, and *Boom!* Other film versions had no input from the playwright.

CHRONOLOGY AND CRITICISMS OF FIFTEEN FILMS

Williams's style of writing worked well for cinema directors. However, two stumbling blocks kept some of these films from being fully realized versions of Williams's work. First, films made in the 1950s and 1960s had to pass through a Hollywood censor's office. Adult dialogue, suggestive material, and visually explicit scenes had to be edited or cut out. Movie ratings did not exist as we know them today. Second, some of Williams's poetic imagery and surrealistic interior monologues worked best on stage. There we accept people expressing themselves in an unreal manner. When blown up into a huge, realistic image on a movie screen, these kinds of self-expression can lose the playwright's meaning.

A quick critique of these films will show how they succeeded in capturing the dramatic qualities Williams intended. Film critic and historian Leonard Maltin is used as the primary consultant to document the films.

The Glass Menagerie (1950)

Hollywood's first try at filming a Williams play starred Gertrude Lawrence as Amanda, Kirk Douglas as Tom, and Jane Wyman as Laura. Williams did not work on this script. He indicated he did not think this film captured the essence of the play and was furious at some of the censorship. The story was remade as a TV film in 1973, starring Katharine Hepburn as Amanda, Sam Waterston as Tom, and Joanna Miles as Laura. This film, directed by Anthony Harvey, was adapted by Williams. Maltin called it the "superior version."[1] In 1987, Paul Newman directed his wife, Joanne Woodward, as Amanda, John Malkovich as Tom, and Karen Allen as Laura in the latest film version.

A Streetcar Named Desire (1951)

Directed by Elia Kazan and scripted by Williams and Oscar Saul, this excellent recreation pushed Hollywood to new heights in adult material. In fact, critic R. Barton Palmer makes a case for *Streetcar* as the first true adult film made by mainstream Hollywood. "With its revelation and dramatization of sexual misconduct, its delineation of a horrifying descent into madness, its portrayal of women driven and even controlled by desire, the play offered themes that could not be accommodated" by the usual 1950 women's film with a happy ending.[2] It allowed adult filmgoers to use their intellects and understanding of two leading characters, Stanley and Blanche, who are made up of both sympathetic and unsympathetic elements. It also studied the power and destructive nature of desire in a totally adult manner.

Marlon Brando as Stanley, Kim Hunter as Stella, Vivien Leigh as Blanche, and Karl Malden as Mitch gave "flawless performances." The movie received a record twelve Academy Award nominations, including Best Picture. Hunter, Leigh, and Malden won Oscars.[3] This play was remade for television in 1984, starring Ann-Margret as Blanche, Treat Williams as Stanley, Beverly D'Angelo as Stella, and Randy Quaid as Mitch. Outstanding acting makes "this version stand proudly beside its classic predecessor."[4]

The Rose Tattoo (1955)

Williams's friend Italian actress Anna Magnani was not a clear enough English speaker to land the Broadway role of Serefina. However, director Daniel Mann cast her in his film version. He worked with Magnani on dialogue, and saw her win the Academy Award for Best Actress. Burt Lancaster played Alvaro, and Oscar nominee Marisa Pavan played the teenage daughter Rosa. The film was nominated for Best Picture. James Wong Howe won for Best Cinematography.

Baby Doll (1956)

Williams wrote the screenplay with Elia Kazan as director. The film caused a furor for its sexual tension. Carroll Baker played the lead and won an Oscar nomination. Karl Malden played her husband. Mildred Dunnock won an Oscar nomination for the aging servant based on Aunt Rose. Eli Wallach and Rip Torn made their film debuts. Unusual for its time was the stark, black-and-white on-location filming.

Cat on a Hot Tin Roof (1958)

Director Richard Brooks and James Poe wrote the adaptation. Elizabeth Taylor was cast as Maggie, Paul Newman as Brick, Burl Ives as Big Daddy, and Judith Anderson as Big Mama. Maltin said this "classic study of mendacity comes to the screen somewhat laundered but still packing a wallop."[5] The film was nominated for Oscars as Best

Picture, Best Actor, Best Actress, and Best Director—but none were winners.

Suddenly Last Summer (1959)

Williams's friend Gore Vidal was chosen to be the co-screenwriter. Joseph L. Mankiewicz directed. Katharine Hepburn as the wealthy, wicked Violet, and Elizabeth Taylor as her disturbed niece Catharine both got Best Actress nominations. This difficult, multilayered story with elements of sexual perversion, guilt, madness, and murder by cannibalism was difficult to film. An excellent British film was made for television in 1992 starring Maggie Smith as Violet and Natasha Richardson as her niece. Maltin said the British version is what "the white-washed . . . version should have been had screen morals of the time not intervened."[6]

The Fugitive Kind (1959)

In spite of its cast of greatly experienced Williams players (Anna Magnani, Marlon Brando, Joanne Woodward, and Maureen Stapleton), and Williams as coauthor of the screenplay, the public did not support this film. Even the work of fine director Sidney Lumet did not make the film a financial success. Some critics, such as Bosley Crowther of *The New York Times*, felt it was an excellent version of his play, *Orpheus Descending*.

123

The Roman Spring of Mrs. Stone (1961)

This film was made from Williams's novel of the same name, and it was reported to be his favorite. Although Lotte Lenya was nominated for Best Supporting Actress, the film's star, Vivien Leigh as Mrs. Stone, was passed over for nomination.

Summer and Smoke (1961)

Starring Geraldine Page, Laurence Harvey, and Rita Moreno, the film adaptation of the play, set in 1916 Mississippi, had what Maltin called torrid performances. Alma was a great role for Ms. Page, who starred in the off-Broadway revival and received an Academy Award nomination for the film.

Sweet Bird of Youth (1962)

This film has strong performances by Geraldine Page as Alexandra the fading movie star, Paul Newman as Chance her gigolo, with supporting roles by Shirley Knight and Ed Begley as the corrupt town boss. Page and Knight received nominations for Best Actress and Supporting Actress, and Begley won the Oscar for Best Supporting Actor. It was written and directed by Richard Brooks.

Period of Adjustment (1962)

Williams called this play "A Serious Comedy." Jane Fonda and Jim Hutton played the newlyweds, with Lois Nettleton and Tony Franciosa acting the older troubled couple they try to support. The director was George Roy Hill.

The Night of the Iguana (1964)

Veteran director John Huston took on this troubling tale. Richard Burton was cast as Reverend Shannon, Deborah Kerr as Hannah, Ava Gardner as Maxine, and Grayson Hall as Judith Fellows, the character who led the tour with Shannon. Grayson Hall won the Oscar for Best Supporting Actress, and costumer Dorothy Jeakins won her field's Oscar. Burton was already nominated that year for his lead role in *Becket*.

Ten Blocks on the Camino Real (1966)

Director Jack Landau filmed this play for the National Educational Television network. Starring young Martin Sheen as Kilroy, this expressionistic, sometimes surreal film also gives writing credit to Tennessee Williams, but it is unclear how much he contributed.

This Property is Condemned (1966)

Fine performers Mary Badham, Natalie Wood, Robert Redford, Kate Reid, Robert Blake, and Charles Bronson, among others, fill out the large cast created from the poignant one-act play. Director Sydney Pollack and screenwriters including Francis Ford Coppola could not make a believable tale out of this slender story of the cruel abandonment of a brave child.

125

Boom! (1968)

British director Joseph Losey used locations in Sardinia and Rome to attempt to make this version of Williams's play *The Milk Train Doesn't Stop Here Anymore* a success. Losey failed. Performers Elizabeth Taylor, Richard Burton, Joanna Shimkus, and playwright Noel Coward could not make a hit of this film of Williams's work.

Although these films are not perfect recreations of Williams's stage productions, they allow students to watch outstanding writers, directors, and designers at work on his material. They show us Williams's enduring characters played by some of the best, highly recognized actors to work in American theater.

RECENT REVIVALS SHOW WILLIAMS'S STAYING POWER

When Williams's plays are revived, critics, actors, and directors all have strong opinions about how they should be done. Often a critical debate explodes. These passionate, conflicting views show how important Williams's plays are in today's theater.

On March 23, 2005, a Broadway revival of *The Glass Menagerie* opened, directed by David Leveaux. An experienced director on London and New York stages, Leveaux decided to cast well-known film stars Jessica Lange as Amanda and Christian Slater as Tom. Lange, slim and attractive in her fifties, easily played the role as if Amanda were about forty-five. Slater had to move between the older Narrator and the twenty-something Tom.

The New York Times critic Ben Brantley did not buy their interpretation. He wrote about the "misdirected and miscast stars: the two-time Oscar winner Jessica Lange, who brings a sleepy neurotic sensuality to the role of the vital and domineering Amanda . . . and Christian Slater, who plays her poetical son Tom as a red-hot roughneck."[7] Critics from *Curtain Up* magazine said: "Despite the actors' often misguided mannerisms and line delivery, and the production's interesting but distracting look, it does all come together . . ."[8]

In an interview for *Playbill*, Lange said of her own plan for the role: "I made a deliberate decision not to play Amanda as some delusional relic of Southern gentility."[9] Lange tried to make her a woman easily understood by downtrodden, midlife mothers of today. Lange had the challenge of impressing critics who had recently seen Sally Field play Amanda in a Kennedy Center hit revival of the show in 2004.

Just as controversial was the revival of *A Streetcar Named Desire* on Broadway in April 2005. This production was directed by another Englishman, Edward Hall. It also featured actors that did not convince all the critics. Playing Blanche, film and stage star Natasha Richardson looked tall, youthful, and strong. Critics wondered why she needed to put paper lanterns over the lightbulbs, since her beauty was hardly fading. Critics also found John C. Reilly to be a stretch for their image of Stanley Kowalski. Eric Grode, critic for *Broadway.com*, said Reilly, who is noted for playing intense losers, "is the unlikeliest Stanley" since a musical cartoon version of the show appeared on *The Simpsons*.[10] Without a primitive, virile Stanley, Grode writes that "the sexual tension between Stanley and Blanche stays at an extremely low simmer."

Other critics praised Richardson (daughter of actress Vanessa Redgrave) for her performance. Critic Malcolm Johnson said that by the final scenes of the play, "Richardson has become Blanche, broken and lost and emotionally short-circuited."[11] Johnson found Reilly's Stanley "bull-like but crafty" and said he "nearly succeeds in putting the shadow of Marlon Brando to rest."[12] Clive Barnes wrote in the *New York Post* that Richardson "is a heaven-sent Blanche—a role she seems to have been born to play . . . her manner a mix of the shy, the sensuous, and the frankly sensual."[13]

About her approach to Blanche, Natasha Richardson said: "In playing someone who's in the midst of such pain and chaos, it's very necessary for me to have stability and order and calm in my own life. I've never before tackled anything of this size or range—period. . . . she is never off-stage except for half a scene!"[14]

Theater director Michael Wilson has made it a career commitment to revive the works of Tennessee Williams. Previously a director at the Alley Theatre of Houston, Texas, Wilson has been at the helm of the Hartford Stage

Company since 1998. During all these years, Wilson has worked with Christopher Baker, a classically trained *dramaturg*. This is an important position of support in the professional theater.

In letters and a personal interview conducted during December 2005, Baker explained his role as dramaturg: "What I have done in most plays is the production history, so that I give everyone else what has been done with this play before, and the critical history, so we know and can read what has been said about it before. We have that going in. I then do an annotated version of the script. I clear up any question about a locale, or something said in the play. Those are things I do before we start work."

DRAMATURG—*Member of a theater organization that prepares the script for performance regarding translations, updated versions, and historical background. During production, the dramaturg advises directors and designers about the playwright's intentions.*

When asked if he facilitated the sharing of ideas between director and designers, Baker said: "We do all sit down and have sessions together, especially on Williams. . . . It's me being another smarty pants in the room, but one who does not then have to do anything. I can come at it from an academic point of view, and an audience point of view."[15]

Baker explained that Michael Wilson is doing what he called a Williams marathon. He produces a work by Williams each year. "The idea was to alternate each season

Author Spring Hermann interviews dramaturg Christopher Baker about the Hartford stage production of *A Lovely Sunday for Creve Coeur* in March 2006.

between a popular title and a lesser known one . . . our audience became well-versed in the plays. Michael thought this endeavor important because as far as we know, this retrospective has not been attempted for a great American writer, in particular, Williams."[16]

Michael Wilson was set to direct Williams's *A Lovely Sunday for Creve Coeur* at the Hartford Stage in the spring of 2006. In December 2005, Baker discussed how he was helping Wilson plan to do this seldom seen work. First, he was researching every draft of the play, as well as studying the 1979 published version when it played off Broadway. Baker explained their goal was to get the most authentic script possible.

"*Creve Coeur* has at least two or three versions. There is also a screenplay. When you look at Williams's archives, he wrote draft after draft," Baker said. Baker was betting he would find an alternative draft in the Williams archives at Butler Library, Columbia University in New York, a version that was "much less realistic" than the published version.

When asked how Williams's works are protected and released, Baker explained: "The University of the South (in Tennessee) is the Williams estate—they are the rights holder." Williams set this up in his will. However, the University of the South uses a London theatrical agency to negotiate the rights to do a Williams play. Baker said that this agency "is very supportive and realistic about the rights."

Once Baker and the agency agreed on the exact

manuscript changes, a basic script still needed to be purchased. The Samuel French Publishing Company supplied the actual scripts, charged per performance, and returned the royalties after their share to the estate. These complicated arrangements are not only common with Williams. They can happen with any playwright whose works are under copyright.

Tennessee Williams would have been pleased to see his plays continue to intrigue, entertain, and enlighten audiences around the world. Williams's plays are not only revived in North America and Europe but have become popular with Russian audiences. Dramaturg Christopher Baker, who has studied Williams productions in Russia, noted that the playwright is greatly respected in Moscow: "Now that censorship has been lifted, they have readapted his plays. His popularity has a new kick."[17]

Williams only wanted to write and have his writing enjoyed. In the spring of 1982, he wrote to his close friend Maria St. Just who lived in England: "I have a play opening in Chicago on Tuesday [April 27]: am casting another play in New York on the 28th, something for the "Miami Festival"—I have a play that I want to develop, so there I'll go."[18] In May 1982, he complained to St. Just that his American agents were not trying to get him new American productions: "Well, my dear girl, I must suspend these rather bleak communications *pour le moment* and do a bit of work on a play called *The Lingering Hour*— the twilight of the world which I hope I am managing to make somewhat poetic despite its subject matter. With all my love, Tennessee."[19]

Williams never completed this play before he died in February 1983. Yet Williams need not have been concerned about his work being produced in his native country or anywhere else in the theater world. Tennessee Williams said he *was* his work —and his work still lives. His creative genius will certainly draw audiences to stage and screen for many generations to come.

CHRONOLOGY

1911—Thomas Lanier Williams III is born on March 26 in Columbus, Mississippi.

Tom, mother Edwina, and sister Rose live with grandparents while father Cornelius sells on the road.

1914–1915—Reverend Walter and Grandmother Isabel Dakin move to Nashville, Tennessee, and then Clarksdale, Mississippi. Tom and his family come along.

1916—Tom is seriously ill with diphtheria and a kidney infection.

1918—Cornelius Williams moves wife and children to St. Louis permanently.

1919—January: Brother Dakin is born; Edwina contracts influenza.

1920—March: Tom leaves St. Louis to live with grandparents in Clarksdale.

1921—Tom returns to St. Louis to live with parents and completes his schooling. At age twelve, gets his first typewriter.

1925—Rose is sent to Vicksburg for private school; onset of her behavior and emotional problems.

1927—Tom wins first writing award, from *Smart Set* magazine.

1928—Tom is taken on European tour with grandfather. *Weird Tales* magazine buys his first story.

1929—Fall: Tom enrolls in University of Missouri at Columbia. Audits playwriting class; studies dramatists; completes three years. Publishes poetry.

1931—Thanksgiving at home: Tom's parents fight so vehemently that he asks mother to throw father out. Summer: Clerks at International Shoe.

1932—Summer: Tom is forced to quit University of Missouri. He works again as a clerk for International Shoe, on and off for several years.

1935—Tom suffers collapse from exhaustion, nerves, and depression. Resigns from International Shoe; spends six months with grandparents in Memphis; has first short play produced in June.

1936—Enrolls at Washington University in St. Louis, studies literature. One-act play is produced by Webster Groves Theatre Guild.

1937—Tom completes degree at University of Iowa. Takes theater courses.

Completes two full-length plays in workshop. Applies for scholarship to return. Chair of the University of Iowa theater department refuses him.

December: The Mummers theater in St. Louis produces *The Fugitive Kind*.

1938—Revises his full-length play, *Not About Nightingales*, set in a prison. (Not produced until 1998.)

1939—Lives in New Orleans, starts sending out stories and plays as "Tennessee Williams."

1940—January: Accepted in New School's Dramatic Workshop, New York. Writes *Battle of Angels*; works on *Stairs to the Roof*.

1941—*Battle of Angels* gets first professional production in Boston, but fails.

1942–1944—Writes plays; lives off grants, part-time jobs, one stint as Hollywood scriptwriter, charity of family and friends.

1944—Grandmother Dakin dies.

December: *The Glass Menagerie* opens in Chicago.

1945—*The Glass Menagerie* is a hit on Broadway. Works on *A Streetcar Named Desire*, *Stairs to the Roof*.

1946—Works on *A Streetcar Named Desire*, *Summer and Smoke*, *Camino Real*.

1947—July: *Summer and Smoke* opens in Dallas. *Stairs to the Roof* opens at Pasadena Playhouse, California.

December: *A Streetcar Named Desire* opens on Broadway. Wins Pulitzer and New York Drama

Critics Circle award. Parents permanently separate.

1948—January–August: Tours Europe, writes.

October: *Summer and Smoke* opens on Broadway.

Frank Merlo becomes Williams's assistant and lover for fourteen years.

1949—January–August: Williams tours Europe with Merlo, writes.

Fall: Discovers Key West, writes *The Rose Tattoo*.

1950—June–August: Tours Europe with Merlo. *The Roman Spring of Mrs. Stone* published.

December: *The Rose Tattoo* opens in Chicago. Film of *The Glass Menagerie* released.

1951—February: *The Rose Tattoo* opens on Broadway. Wins Tony Award.

1952—Film of *A Streetcar Named Desire* is released. Works on *Camino Real*. *Summer and Smoke* runs off Broadway.

June–September: Lives in Rome and Paris with Merlo.

Winter in Key West with Grandfather Dakin.

1953—*Camino Real* opens on Broadway. Writes *Cat on a Hot Tin Roof*.

Lives in Europe, New York, New Orleans, and Key West.

1954—June–September lives in Rome.

Fall: *The Rose Tattoo* films in Key West.

1955—February: Grandfather Dakin dies.

March: *Cat on a Hot Tin Roof* opens on Broadway.

June–September: Travels without Merlo through Europe, begins taking drugs.

Fall: In New York; writes screenplay for *Baby Doll*.

Film of *The Rose Tattoo* is released.

1956—*Sweet Bird of Youth* opens in Miami.

Summer: Serious trouble with Merlo, Williams near nervous breakdown.

Fall: Mother is committed to psychiatric ward; Williams flees to Virgin Islands.

1957—January: Keeps mother in Key West; writes *Orpheus Descending*.

May: Cornelius Williams dies. Williams deeply affected.

September: Undergoes psychotherapy in New York.

1958—January: *Something Unspoken* and *Suddenly Last Summer* open off Broadway.

June: Breaks with psychiatrist, goes to Europe. Writes *Period of Adjustment*.

Film of *Cat on a Hot Tin Roof* is released.

1959—March: *Sweet Bird of Youth* opens on Broadway.

April: *I Rise in Flames, Cried the Phoenix* opens off Broadway.

Travels through Europe with Merlo. Film of *Suddenly Last Summer* released.

1960—Writes *The Night of the Iguana* in Key West. Travels with mother and Dakin to L.A.

November: *Period of Adjustment* opens on Broadway.

Film of *Orpheus Descending*, called *The Fugitive Kind*, released.

1961—Spends year writing, traveling in Europe.

December: *The Night of the Iguana* opens on Broadway.

1962—*The Milk Train Doesn't Stop Here* opens at Spoleto Festival.

Films of *Sweet Bird of Youth* and *Period of Adjustment* are released.

1963—Merlo is ill. *Milk Train Doesn't Stop Here* opens off Broadway.

September: Merlo dies of cancer in New York.

1964—Lives in Key West, severely depressed. Writes *Slapstick Tragedy*.

Film of *The Night of the Iguana* released.

1965—Summer: Moves to New York with paid male companion.

1966—*Slapstick Tragedy* opens in New York.

1968—*The Seven Descents of Myrtle* opens on Broadway. Film of *The Milk Train Doesn't Stop Here*, called *BOOM!*, is released.

1969—Mental health declines. Dakin has Williams baptized Catholic in Key West.

Spring: Failed suicide attempt with sleeping pills.

In the Bar of a Tokyo Hotel opens in New York.

November: Has a breakdown. Dakin commits Williams to St. Louis hospital for detoxification and psychiatric treatment.

1970—Back in Key West, continues to write. Paranoia develops.

1971—Breaks with thirty-two-year agent, Audrey Wood. *Out Cry* opens in Chicago, then in New York.

1972—*Small Craft Warnings* opens off Broadway. Williams sometimes plays a role.

1973—March: *Out Cry* opens in New York. Spends year touring Far East.

1974—*Out Cry* opens off Broadway, but fails. Broadway revival of *Cat on a Hot Tin Roof* is huge success.

1975—Four major revivals are hits in New York and Washington.

Works on *Red Devil Battery Sign*; briefly produced in Boston. Williams's book *Memoirs* is published.

1976—November: *Eccentricities of a Nightingale* opens in New York, but fails.

December: Made lifetime member of American Academy of Arts and Letters.

1977—*Vieux Carre* opens on Broadway, but fails. *Red Devil Battery Sign* opens in London.

1978—*Vieux Carre* is a hit in London; *A Lovely Sunday for Creve Coeur* opens in Charleston festival.

1979—*A Lovely Sunday for Creve Coeur* opens off Broadway.

December 2: Williams receives the Kennedy Center Award for the Arts.

1980—*Clothes for a Summer Hotel* opens on Broadway.

June: Mother dies at age ninety-five.

Receives Presidential Medal of Freedom, highest civilian award.

Becomes Distinguished Writer in Residence at University of British Columbia.

1981—*Something Cloudy, Something Clear*, an autobiographical play, opens off Broadway successfully.

Receives the third annual Common Wealth Award in New York.

1982—*A House Not Meant to Stand* opens in Chicago.

June: Honorary Doctor of Letters degree from Harvard. Spends summer abroad with a new male friend who reminds him of Merlo.

Works on adaptation of *The Seagull* by Chekhov, other new works.

1983—Living at Hotel Elysee in New York, working, but suffering depression.

February 24 or 25: Dies in hotel suite, with medicine bottle top lodged in throat.

Death judged an accident.

Broadway theaters all dimmed their lights in his memory.

1994—Honored by a U.S. Postal Service stamp, after the required ten-year wait after death.

CHAPTER NOTES

CHAPTER 1. A PLAYWRIGHT IS BORN

1. Donald Spoto, *The Kindness of Strangers: The Life of Tennessee Williams* (Boston: Little, Brown and Company, 1985), p. 55.

2. Albert J. Devlin, ed., *Conversations With Tennessee Williams* (Jackson, Miss.: University Press of Mississippi, 1986), p. 17.

3. Lyle Leverich, *Tom: The Unknown Tennessee Williams* (New York: W. W. Norton & Company, 1995), p. 226.

4. Tennessee Williams, *The Fugitive Kind*, ed., with an introduction by Allean Hale (New York: New Directions Books, University of the South, 2001), p. 106.

5. Ibid., p. 124.

6. Ibid., p. 132.

7. Ibid., p. xix.

8. Leverich, p. 250.

CHAPTER 2. THE TROUBLED WILLIAMS FAMILY

1. Donald Spoto, *The Kindness of Strangers: The Life of Tennessee Williams* (Boston: Little, Brown and Company, 1985), p. 6.

2. Ronald Hayman, *Tennessee Williams: Everyone Else Is an Audience* (Yale University Press, 1993), p. 5

3. Ibid.

4. Lyle Leverich, *Tom: The Unknown Tennessee Williams* (New York: W. W. Norton & Company, 1995), p. 37.

5. Ibid., p. 38.

6. Hayman, p. 9.

7. Spoto, p. 15.

8. Ibid.

9. Hayman, p. 18.

10. Leverich, p. 65.

11. Tennessee Williams, *In the Winter of Cities* (New York: New Directions, 1952), p. 76.

12. Leverich, p. 89.

13. Ibid., p. 101.

14. Spoto, p. 35.

15. Ibid., p. 40.

16. Leverich, p. 160.

17. Ibid., p. 48.

18. Ibid., p. 153.

19. Ibid., pp. 239–240.

20. Hayman, p. 53.

21. Spoto, p. 77.

22. Leverich, p. 436.

CHAPTER 3. A NEW STYLE OF DRAMA

1. Tennessee Williams, *Memoirs* (New York: Doubleday & Company, 1975), p. 85.

2. Robert A. Martin, ed., reviews reprinted in *Critical Essays on Tennessee Williams* (New York: G. K. Hall & Company, 1997), p. 67.

3. Esther M. Jackson, "Tennessee Williams: The Idea of a 'Plastic Form,'" reprinted in *Critical Essays on Tennessee Williams*, ed. by Robert A. Martin (New York: G. K. Hall & Company, 1997), p. 197.

4. Williams, *Memoirs*, pp. 84–85.

5. Albert J. Devlin, ed., *Conversations With Tennessee Williams*, (Jackson, Miss.: University Press of Mississippi, 1986), p. 10.

6. Tennessee Williams, *The Glass Menagerie*, in *The*

Theatre of Tennessee Williams, vol. 1 (New York: New Directions Books, 1971), p. 163.

7. Williams, *Memoirs*, p. 48.

8. Williams, *The Glass Menagerie*, p. 159.

9. Ibid., p. 237.

10. Ibid., p. 228.

11. Ibid., p. 164.

12. Lincoln Barnett, "Tennessee Williams," *Life*, February 16, 1948, p. 116.

13. Roger Boxill, *Tennessee Williams* (New York: St. Martins Press, 1987), p. 22.

14. Judith J. Thompson, *Tennessee Williams' Plays: Memory, Myth, and Symbol* (New York: Peter Lang Publishing, 1989), p. 14.

15. Martin, pp. 19–24.

Chapter 4. Dark Desire

1. Donald Spoto, *The Kindness of Strangers: The Life of Tennessee Williams* (Boston: Little, Brown and Company, 1985), p. 118.

2. Ronald Hayman, *Tennessee Williams: Everyone Else Is an Audience* (Yale University Press, 1993), p. 103.

3. Tennessee Williams, *Memoirs* (New York: Doubleday & Company, 1975), p. 131.

4. Louise Blackwell, "Tennessee Williams and the Predicament of Women," in *Tennessee Williams: A Collection of Essays*, Stephen S. Stanton, ed. (Upper Saddle River, N.J.: PrenticeHall, Inc., 1977), p. 100.

5. Chris Jones, "Sex in the Big Easy," *Front & Center Magazine*, Spring 2005, p. 6.

6. Ibid.

7. Tennessee Williams, *A Streetcar Named Desire*, *Theatre of Tennessee Williams*, vol. 1 (New York: New Directions Books, 1971), p. 323.

8. Ibid., p. 351.

9. Ibid., p. 332.

10. Judith J. Thompson, *Tennessee Williams' Plays: Memory, Myth, and Symbol* (New York: Peter Lang Publishing, 1989), p. 41.

11. Williams, *A Streetcar Named Desire*, p. 323.

12. Kimball King, "The Rebirth of Orpheus Descending," in *Critical Essays on Tennessee Williams*, Robert A. Martin, ed. (New York: G. K. Hall & Company, 1997), p. 140.

13. Robert A. Martin, ed., reviews reprinted in *Critical Essays on Tennessee Williams* (New York: G. K. Hall & Company, 1997), pp. 25–30.

14. Williams, *Memoirs*, p. 156.

15. Spoto, p. 153.

16. *Five O'Clock Angel: Letters of Tennessee Williams to Maria St. Just 1948–1982*, with commentary by Maria St. Just (New York: Alfred A. Knopf, 1990), p. 14.

17. Hayman, p. 131.

18. Donald Windham, ed., *Tennessee Williams's Letters to Donald Windham 1940–1965* (University of Georgia Press, 1996), p. 249.

CHAPTER 5. DECEPTION AND GREED

1. Arthur B. Waters, "Tennessee Williams: Ten Years Later," *Conversations with Tennessee Williams*, Albert J. Devlin, ed. (Jackson, Miss.: University Press of Mississippi, 1986), p. 35.

2. Ibid.

3. Tennessee Williams, *Cat on a Hot Tin Roof, Theatre of Tennessee Williams*, Vol. III (New York: New Directions Books, 1975), p. 117.

4. Ibid., p. 119.

5. Ibid.

6. Ibid., p. 26.

7. Ibid., p. 53.

8. Dianne Cafagna, "Blanche DuBois and Maggie the Cat: Illusion and Reality in Tennessee Williams," in *Critical Essays on Tennessee Williams*, ed. Robert A. Martin (New York: G. K. Hall & Company, 1997), p. 122.

9. Williams, *Cat on a Hot Tin Roof*, p. 61.

10. Ibid., p. 124.

11. Judith J. Thompson, *Tennessee Williams' Plays: Memory, Myth, and Symbol* (New York: Peter Lang Publishing, 1989), p. 81.

12. Brooks Atkinson, "Theatre: Tennessee Williams's 'Cat,'" *The New York Times*, March 25, 1955, p. 18.

13. Ibid.

14. Robert Coleman, *New York Daily Mirror*, March 25, 1955, p. 21. Reprinted in *Critical Essays on Tennessee Williams*, edited by Robert A. Martin (New York: G. K. Hall & Company, 1997), p. 45.

15. Ibid.

16. "A Curtain Up Review: Cat on a Hot Tin Roof," n.d., <http://www.curtainup.com/catonahottineroof> (August 11, 2006).

CHAPTER 6. BODY AND SOUL

1. Tennessee Williams, *Something Cloudy, Something Clear* (New York: New Directions, 1995), p. 23.

2. Thomas P. Adler, "Before the Fall—and After," *The Cambridge Companion to Tennessee Williams*, Matthew C. Roudane, ed. (Cambridge University Press, 1997), p. 116.

3. Tennessee Williams, *Summer and Smoke, The Theatre of Tennessee Williams*, vol. II (New York: New Directions Books, 1971), p. 202.

4. Ibid., p. 221.

5. Ibid., p. 241.

6. Brooks Atkinson, *The New York Times*, October 7, 1948, p. 33.

7. Donald Spoto, *The Kindness of Strangers: The Life of*

Tennessee Williams (Boston: Little, Brown and Company, 1985), pp. 179–180.

8. Brooks Atkinson, *New York Times*, February 5, 1951, p. 33.

9. Ibid.

10. Tennessee Williams, *Night of the Iguana*, *The Theatre of Tennessee Williams*, vol. IV (New York: New Directions Books, 1972), p. 302.

11. Ibid., p. 373.

12. Howard Taubman, "Theatre: *Night of the Iguana* Opens." *The New York Times*, December 29, 1961, p. 10.

13. Williams, *Summer and Smoke*, p. 243.

14. Williams, *Night of the Iguana*, pp. 367–368.

15. Tennessee Williams, "A Summer of Discovery," from *Where I Live: Selected Essays*, eds. Christine R. Day and Bob Woods (New York: New Directions, 1978), p. 123.

CHAPTER 7. SHORT PLAYS AND OTHER WORKS

1. Laura Kepley, speaking at Trinity Repertory Theatre, Providence, Rhode Island, October 29, 2005.

2. Tennessee Williams, *27 Wagons Full of Cotton and Other One-Act Plays* (New York: New Directions, 1945), p. 69.

3. Ibid., p. 70.

4. Ibid., p. 215.

5. Ibid., p. 217.

6. Ibid., p. 190.

7. Ibid., p. 193.

8. Ibid., p. 199.

9. Mel Gussow, "Stage: 'Ten by Tennessee,' Short Williams Plays," May 20, 1986, <http://www.nytimes.com/books/00/12/31/specials/williams-ten.html> (October 22, 2005).

10. Karen Bovard, "Lost in the Funhouse: New Life

for Some Neglected One-Acts by Tennessee Williams," *Hartford Advocate*, October 19, 2003, <http://www.hartfordadvocate.com/gbase/arts> (November 30, 2005).

11. Tennessee Williams, Foreword to *Camino Real* (New York: New Directions, 1953), p. ix.

12. Tennessee Williams, *Memoirs* (New York: Doubleday and Company, 1975), p. 189.

13. Ibid., p. 194.

14. Ibid., p. 203.

15. Tennessee Williams, *Small Craft Warnings* (New Directions, 1970), p. 15.

16. Tennessee Williams, *Red Devil Battery Sign* (New Directions, 1975), p. 62.

17. Albert J. Devlin, ed., "Roundtable: Tennessee Williams, Craig Anderson, and T. E. Kalem Talk About Creve Coeur," *Conversations With Tennessee Williams* (Jackson, Miss.: University Press of Mississippi, 1986), p. 310.

18. Ibid., p. 311.

19. Ibid., p. 313.

20. Ibid., p. 316.

21. Dotson Rader, *Tennessee: Cry of the Heart* (New York: Doubleday & Company, 1985), p. 298.

22. Ibid., p. 360.

CHAPTER 8. OTHER PLAYWRIGHTS

1. Tennessee Williams, *Memoirs* (New York: Doubleday and Company, 1975), p. 41.

2. Ibid., p. 40.

3. Ibid., p. 41.

4. Oscar Brockett and Robert J. Ball, *The Essential Theatre*, 8th ed. (Wadsworth/Thompson Learning Inc., 2004), p. 165.

5. Peter Arnott, *The Theatre in Its Time* (Boston: Little, Brown & Company, 1981), p. 366.

6. Dotson Rader, *Tennessee: Cry of the Heart* (New York: Doubleday and Company, 1985), p. 285.

7. "About William Inge," *William Inge Center for the Arts*, n.d., <http://www.ingecenter.org/aboutinge.html> (November 4, 2005).

8. Ibid., p. 1

9. Rader, p. 326.

10. Ronald Hayman, *Tennessee Williams: Everyone Else Is an Audience* (Yale University Press, 1993) p. 98.

11. Raymond Williams, "Arthur Miller: An Overview," *Arthur Miller*, Harold Bloom, ed. (New York: Chelsea House Publishers, 1987), p. 13.

12. Mel Gussow, *Edward Albee: A Singular Journey* (New York: Simon & Schuster, 1999), p. 92.

13. "An Interview With Edward Albee," by Charles S. Krohn and Julian N. Wasserman, March 18, 1981, published in *Edward Albee: An Interview and Essays* (Houston, Tex.: The University of St. Thomas, 1983), p. 2.

14. Edward Albee, *Who's Afraid of Virginia Woolf?* (New York: Atheneum, 1978), pp. 190–191.

CHAPTER 9. WILLIAMS LIVES ON

1. Leonard Maltin, ed., *Leonard Maltin's Movie & Video Guide 1997 Edition* (New York: Signet Books, 1996), p. 509.

2. R. Barton Palmer, "Hollywood in Crisis: Tennessee Williams and the Evolution of the Adult Film," *The Cambridge Companion to Tennessee Williams*, Matthew C. Roudane, ed. (Cambridge University Press, 1997), p. 214.

3. *Leonard Maltin's Movie & Video Guide*, p. 1285.

4. Ibid.

5. Ibid., p. 213.

6. Ibid., p. 1293.

7. Ben Brantley, "Theatre Review: A 'Menagerie' Full of Stars, Sillouettes, and Weird Sounds," n.d., <http://

theatre2nytimes.com/mem/theater/review> (May 13, 2005).

8. "A Curtain Up Review: *The Glass Menagerie*," n.d., <http://www.curtainup.com/glassmenageriebway> (May 13, 2005).

9. C. F. Kane, "Amanda for All Seasons," *Playbill*, March 2005, p. 54.

10. Eric Grode, *A Streetcar Named Desire*, n.d., <http://www.broadway.com/gen/Buzz> (May 13, 2005).

11. Ibid.

12. Malcolm Johnson, "Close to Solving the Brando Problem," *Hartford Courant*, April 27, 2005, p. D4.

13. Clive Barnes, *A Streetcar Named Desire*, n.d., <http://www.broadway.com/gen/Buzz_Story> p. 1 (May 13, 2005).

14. Jerry Tallmer, "Darkness Becomes Her," in *Playbill*, April 2005, p. 26.

15. Christopher Baker, interview with the author, at the Hartford Stage Company, Hartford, Conn., December 20, 2005.

16. Christopher Baker, in a letter to the author, December 16, 2005.

17. Baker, interview with the author.

18. *Five O'Clock Angel: Letters of Tennessee Williams to Maria St. Just 1948–1982* (New York: Alfred A. Knopf, 1990), p. 388.

19. Ibid., p. 390.

GLOSSARY

detoxification—A medical program to purify the body of toxins, especially drugs and alcohol.

diphtheria—A contagious bacterial disease that attacks the throat, nose, nerves, and heart. Children are now vaccinated against it.

dramaturg—Member of a theater organization that prepares the script for performance regarding translations, updated versions, and historical background. During production, the dramaturg advises directors and designers about the playwright's intentions.

irony—The incongruity of an expected situation (or its outcome) and the actual situation (or its outcome). In language, irony is the deliberate use of words to contrast an apparent meaning with the words' intended meaning (which are usually the complete opposite of each other).

mendacity—Untruthfulness, dishonesty.

metaphor—An implied comparison achieved by using a word or phrase not in its literal sense, but as an analogy. Example (from Shakespeare): "Life's but a walking shadow, a poor player that struts and frets his hour upon the stage."

monologue (internal or interior)—A long speech by an individual character in which he lets the audience alone know his inner thoughts and feelings.

monologue (external or exterior)—A long speech by an individual character, sometimes in the presence of other characters, that reveals his past or planned actions and intentions.

paranoia—Excessive anxiety and fear about one's own person, to the point of being psychotic.

pathos—An element in creative art or experience that evokes sympathy, pity, and/or compassion.

realism—A style of writing in which the subject is represented as it would be in real life.

symbol—Something that stands for, represents, or suggests another thing.

symbolism—The representation of things by use of symbols.

theme—A distinctive quality or concern in one or more works of fiction.

Major Works of
Tennessee
Williams

The Fugitive Kind (1937)

Not About Nightingales (1938; produced 1998)

Battle of Angels (1941)

The Glass Menagerie (1944)

Summer and Smoke (1947)

Stairs to the Roof (1947)

A Streetcar Named Desire (1947)

The Rose Tattoo (1950)

The Roman Spring of Mrs. Stone (1950)

Camino Real (1953)

Cat on a Hot Tin Roof (1955)

Baby Doll (1955)

Sweet Bird of Youth (1956)

Orpheus Descending (1957)

Something Unspoken (1958)

Suddenly Last Summer (1958)

Period of Adjustment (1958)

I Rise in Flames, Cried the Phoenix (1959)

The Night of the Iguana (1960)

The Milk Train Doesn't Stop Here (1962)

Slapstick Tragedy (1964)

The Seven Descents of Myrtle (1968)

BOOM! (1968)

In the Bar of a Tokyo Hotel (1969)

Out Cry (1971)

Small Craft Warnings (1972)

Memoirs (1975)

Eccentricities of a Nightingale (1976)

Vieux Carre (1977)

Red Devil Battery Sign (1977)

A Lovely Sunday for Creve Coeur (1978)

Clothes for a Summer Hotel (1980)

Something Cloudy, Something Clear (1981)

A House Not Meant to Stand (1982)

FURTHER READING

Books

Devlin, Albert J. *Conversations With Tennessee Williams.* University Press of Mississippi, 1986.

Roudané, Matthew C. *The Cambridge Companion to Tennessee Williams.* Boston: Cambridge University Press, 1998.

Spoto, Donald, ed. *The Kindness of Strangers: The Life of Tennessee Williams.* De Capo Press, 1997.

Tischler, Nancy M. *Student Companion to Tennessee Williams.* Westport, Conn.: Greenwood Press, 2000.

Internet Addresses

The Tennessee Williams/New Orleans Literary Festival
http://www.tennesseewilliams.net/

The Mississippi Writers Page: Tennessee Williams
http://www.olemiss.edu/depts/english/ms-writers/dir/williams_tennessee/

American Masters: Tennessee Williams
http://www.pbs.org/wnet/americanmasters/database/williams_t.html

INDEX